Anstey's Boundary Disputes 346·410432

D1330086

£22·50

Anstey's Boundary Disputes

and how to resolve them!

Updated by David Powell

THIRD EDITION

N346.410432
430206

Published by RICS Business Services Limited
a wholly owned subsidiary of
The Royal Institution of Chartered Surveyors
under the RICS Books imprint
Surveyor Court
Westwood Business Park
Coventry CV4 8JE
UK

ISBN 1 84219 189 6

First edition October 1990
Second edition February 1998

Illustrations by Michael Cromar

A proportion of the royalties from the sale of this book go to the John
Anstey Foundation, a charitable trust.

Typeset by Columns Design Ltd., Reading
Printed in Great Britain by JW Arrowsmith, Bristol

Contents

 # Introduction

Most boundary disputes take place in suburban back gardens. Most of them could easily be avoided. Most are quite simple for two surveyors to solve (or one surveyor instructed jointly). Most clients refuse to accept what their surveyors tell them.

If you think that the sweeping generalisations above are untrue, then you have almost certainly not had a typical boundary dispute to settle. When it comes to back gardens – or front gardens for that matter – the old Scottish proverb 'Mony a mickle maks a muckle' may be rendered as 'Every mickle maks a muckle'. While most of us live side by side without any difficulties, there are a significant number of people who have problems with the neighbours. Many of these problems are caused by uncertainty over the whereabouts of the legal boundary in relation to a fence, a wall or a hedge.

John Anstey – the original author of this book – did not (always) claim to be the world's leading boundary expert, but there is no doubt that he was an expert not only in dealing with the technical aspects of boundary disputes, but also in giving out wise advice and helping to diffuse what, in essence, are 'people problems'.

The new author of this book – David Powell, a chartered land surveyor and member of the Land Registry Rules Committee – would likewise only make the occasional claim to global expertise. However, he is one of those who have followed happily in the path marked out by John. David knew John well, and shared his interest in the 'people factor' when it came to boundary work. Whether the owner of a hotel in Lincoln – whom David and John once kept up to the wee small hours, treating to their tales of warring neighbours – felt the same way, is a different matter.

These (and many other) hours of discussion on boundary matters, added to David's professional expertise, experience of instruction in over 3,000 boundary disputes, and notes from lectures on the subject throughout the UK – and, when he can manage it, in the Caribbean – make David uniquely qualified to add to and update John's work.

Retaining all of John's most useful information, and even most of his asides, this third edition of the book covers some new ground on adverse possession, land registration, the preparation of an expert report and the use of modern measuring techniques. There are two wholly new chapters, on boundaries in housing estates and aerial photography. The new edition also contains even more humorous anecdotes, for the diversion of the readers. With David's updated material interwoven into John's original text, it is hoped that the reader will be able to enjoy the book without worrying about 'who wrote what'.

Despite the frequent occurrence of boundary disputes, particularly in suburbia, there are few practical handbooks written for the layman or the not very experienced surveyor. This book deals with a number of interesting and difficult boundary disputes, and it is hoped that John's tips on how to solve at least the straightforward problems, coupled with the updated and additional information provided by David, will help general practitioners and property owners alike.

Of course, the law will be touched upon, but in fairly simple terms. The law is not a field that surveyors or property owners should get involved in without fully understanding the consequences. For surveyors, it is essential to realise that the law is a subject of its own; surveyors should avoid becoming amateur lawyers, if only for the obvious reason of needing to protect their professional indemnity insurance (PII) cover. Meanwhile, the property owner should understand that while the law is there as a last resort, it is advisable to visit the other resorts first.

The main purpose of this slim volume is to point out the obvious, and one or two less obvious, ways of finding out where a boundary is or was. The book starts with a consideration of deeds, plans and texts; moves on to issues relating to boundaries in walls, houses and streets; takes a brief turn around the garden to examine fences, hedges and ditches; considers methods of measurement and expert report preparation; and ends up in court, which the authors encourage you to avoid entering, but for which eventuality they provide you with some useful pointers – just in case.

Most boundary disputes involve a few inches of land and occur between domestic gardens or commercial buildings. Often the land involved is worthless in monetary terms, but sometimes, in inner-city commercial areas, for example, the land can be extremely valuable indeed.

Lord Hoffman memorably said, during one recent boundary dispute case: 'Claims to small and valueless pieces of land are pressed with the zeal of Fortinbras' army' – and how right he was.

Judge LJ Ward meanwhile lamented, at the beginning of the *Wibberley v Insley* (hedge-and-ditch) Appeal:

'To hear those words "boundary dispute" is to fill a judge even of the most stalwart and amiable disposition with deep foreboding, since disputes between neighbours tend always to compel, as this one did, some unreasonable and extravagant behaviour which profits no one but the lawyers.'

Nevertheless, these problems won't simply go away if professionals ignore them (as one surveyor recently said, 'I hide under my desk when a boundary problem comes in to my office'). Someone has to deal with them and that someone, surely, should be a chartered surveyor who is, after all, used to dealing with people and property on a day-to-day basis.

This book can also be commended to the layman. Many surveyors' workloads these days are such that, if they can give advice down the telephone which saves a potential client from wasting several hundred pounds in employing them to come and tell him that he has no case, they would be delighted to do so. If buying this book helps to save a client from similar expenditure, then it has succeeded in its aim. The purchase of this book is the first rational act in a boundary dispute, and it is to be hoped that the same calm good sense will prevail until the matter is resolved.

One final point. The predominant use of 'he' in this book may tend to suggest that only men are capable of instigating or conducting needlessly acrimonious and overly expensive boundary disputes. However, David wishes to confirm that women are not wholly exempt from this sort of practice. For this reason, it should be noted that the use of the masculine in this book includes the feminine (except, of course, where the authors refer to real people).

Deed plans and Land Registry maps

Do you know where your deed plans are? Do you know what they look like?

If you're involved in any kind of boundary dispute, a perusal of your deeds should be your first act. You will need to find them in order to try to establish where your boundaries actually are.

The majority of property owners do not keep their deeds under the mattress or framed on the dining-room wall (although several do), preferring to trust them to the care of their mortgage lenders. In fact, they might be more secure if they were put up on the wall – the mortgage lenders will not let them out of their vice-like grip until the owner has made the final monthly mortgage payment! A call to the lender, however, followed by the sending of a cheque (usually for less than £50), will procure a photocopy of the deeds.

Before going any further, let's separate deeds from Land Registry (LR) documentation.

Countless numbers of people, when asked to present their deeds, say 'I've got them here!', and proudly hand over their LR documents instead. These are not the deeds. The giveaway is in the name. The LR maintains a *register* of properties (together with other rights, leases, and so on), but it does not *map* land in great detail. The plan attached to the LR documentation, called the 'title plan', is purely a 'where are we?' map. It will show an outline of a property, in red ink, but will not normally contain dimensions, T-marks and other helpful boundary data – for these, you need the deeds.

That is not to say that the LR does not do its utmost to ensure that the title plans for properties fit together like a jigsaw. However, it is the case that the maps underlying the title plans, drawn up by the Ordnance Survey (OS), are simply not up to the job of defining property boundaries down to the last few centimetres.

Why is this the case? Well, OS surveyors have been out mapping the UK for nearly 200 years. They have done (and are still doing) an excellent job. It should be appreciated by all OS map users, though, that the OS is in the business of painting a highly technological and complex picture of the country, and that picture is inevitably full of compromises and quirks. Briefly, the reasons that the LR cannot use OS maps to define boundaries are as follows.

- OS surveyors do not go out deliberately to map private property boundaries (and never have done). They map things (features).

- Where several features are clustered together, for example, a fence, a ditch and a hedge, the OS can only show one of them and the map user can rarely tell which one it is. One of those features may be a boundary feature, or none of them may have anything to do with the boundary, but there will be a solid line on the OS map indicating that there is a feature, or a cluster of features, in the vicinity (see figure 1).

- OS maps have accuracy limitations. These limitations are being reduced as more sophisticated mapping replaces the older versions, but it is still true to say that at 1:1,250 (urban) scale, it is not safe to rely on a scaled measurement as being better than ±1 metre, and at 1:2,500 (rural) scale, the accuracy of a scaled measurement may be no better than ±2.3 metre.

The LR uses OS maps for all its title plans. From the above, it can be seen that it is a futile activity to place a scale rule on a title plan in an attempt to locate the boundary. The LR makes this perfectly clear in its General Boundaries Rule (Section 60 of the *Land Registration Act* 2002).

So, I hear you say, 'if LR title plans are of little use, how **do** I find out where my boundary is?' As the old saying nearly went, 'the answer lies in the deeds', and indeed it should.

Fig. 1

3

The deeds come in a variety of shapes and sizes. They are
the pieces of paper, or linen or pigskin, containing text
and usually (but not always) a plan. They are generally
referred to as '**paper-title**'. Paper-title can be described in
a conveyance, an indenture, an agreement, a
remembrance, a transfer and, no doubt, many other
forms. It is paper-title that describes which bit of land
belongs to the property owner (or lessor, etc).

Thus, in any dispute, the surveyor's first port of call
should always be paper-title.

Interpretation of the text of paper-title is really a matter
for lawyers. There are, for example, phrases in paper title
that can dictate the status of a deed plan, such as 'more
particularly delineated' and 'for the purpose of
identification only', and most surveyors will know that
these words can raise or lower the legal validity of the
measurements that may be written on a deed plan.
However, it is wise to leave this interpretation to the
lawyers and make it clear that you intend to take the
deed plans at face value. The alternative is to take one's
first step into becoming half-surveyor, half-lawyer, a
journey that can only lead to disaster.

It is recognised in the courts that boundary disputes are
difficult and extremely trying affairs, and it is generally
appreciated by judges that surveyors do their best to
locate a boundary by looking at the deed plans. No court
is going to be harsh on a surveyor who has simply tried
to apply the deed plan to the ground without realising
some of the legal nuances of certain forms of words in
the text of a deed. In fact, it is nearly always the case that
lawyers, and judges in particular, are delighted that
surveyors have kept out of the legal bits.

There are some legal words in the form of qualifying phrases that do need to be taken heed of, though, and these include 'approximately', 'a little more a little less' and 'or thereabouts'. These phrases are intended to soften the bite of the dimensions. In other words, if a deed plan shows that the frontage of a property is 60 ft and the wording of the text has one of those qualifying phrases in it, it is pointless for a surveyor to insist that the frontage of the property should be 60 ft 0.000 inches. It is often the case that a measuring tape is suspended between obvious boundary posts at each end of the frontage of a property and the measurement found to be, say, 60 ft 2 inches. There is nothing wrong with that; it is covered by the qualifying phrases in the text of the deed. Surveyors who do not realise this can cause minor skirmishes between neighbours to escalate into full-blown wars. Common-sense should always prevail.

It is also worth reading the text of a deed to see if there are dimensions mentioned that are not on the plan (often the case) or whether clues as to who should plant a hedge or erect a fence are hidden away in obscure corners of the text.

When two or more sets of deeds for neighbouring properties are compared, they often do not match. A surveyor's task in resolving such matters is akin to trying to complete a jigsaw puzzle with no picture on front of the box – with some pieces missing and others that do not fit together when they should. This may sound a hopeless task; however, an experienced boundary surveyor can invariably complete more of the jigsaw than an inexperienced surveyor. One of the purposes of this book is to help readers to become jigsaw experts!

Words or pictures?

One picture is worth a thousand words – except, unfortunately, when one is dealing with legal matters. If the position (or ownership) of a boundary is disputed, surveyors may find themselves having to compare the *words* of a deed with the *pictures* of the attached plan (or of a plan provided separately).

If the words of a deed contradict something shown on a plan attached to it, the words may well prevail. It may be the case that, legally, the plan only governs if the deed specifically so states. It is very important, therefore, to be sure what your starting point is when you set out to decide where a boundary should be.

Don't just unquestioningly accept a plan which your client gives you. Ask to see the deed it belongs to, if there is one. If it doesn't come with a deed, where does it spring from? Does anyone on the other side accept it as a true record, so that any argument is only about interpretation, or is the provenance of the plan itself in dispute?

As this book is not really about how to settle boundary disputes, but how to avoid them or nip them in the bud, this is not the place to lecture you on the proper form of words that must exist in a deed to ensure that the plan has the right status. Suffice to say that if this is a matter that is crucial to the dispute, then it is vital to consult a good property solicitor for a legal interpretation. It is even acceptable for *both* sides' deeds to be sent off (by a chartered surveyor) to a single barrister for 'counsel's opinion'. This can often prevent a dispute escalating purely because the legal status of the plan is not known.

Landlord and tenant plans are notorious for their inaccuracy. Internal office partitions, for example, are often erected without any reference to the legal plan, and it is not unknown for the boundary of one firm's lease to pass through another firm's office furniture. As long as everyone is living and working happily side by side, this does not matter, but if one or other of the parties starts getting the lease plans out, then a long war of attrition may ensue – usually caused by the poor quality of the plans themselves.

David was once involved in a case in a heartbreakingly beautiful part of rural France, where two couples from England had bought a large farmhouse which they wished to use for their regular holidays. They had an agreement drawn up saying who owned what, and then, within six months, they fell out and wished to have the demarcation line within the house marked out by a line of red paint.

The deed (agreement) plan for the farmhouse was not only of very poor quality, being out of scale and drawn by someone who clearly had not measured the farmhouse in the first place, but the line of demarcation represented a width of about one metre on the ground. David realised very quickly that the line passed diagonally across one of the bathrooms – indeed, through the bathroom itself.

Aware that the already Pinteresque atmosphere in the farmhouse would descend into the ice age if he drew his red line across the bathroom floor, around the plastic ducks and through the bathtub itself, David suggested that he should, instead, measure up the farmhouse, draw up a fresh plan showing what actually existed in the right place, and then redraw the demarcation line on the plan so that it ran along walls rather than through rooms. The parties agreed and David spent a happy week measuring-up.

In the interests of impartiality, David suggested to his joint clients that he should stay at an auberge in the local village rather than in the farmhouse itself (on one side or other of the demarcation line!), a suggestion that also enabled him to learn much about the product of the local vineyards. Boundary disputes do sometimes have their advantages.

Applying paper-title to the land in question

Having studied the deeds to a property, everything may seem clear and simple. However, difficulties are often encountered when attempting to *apply* those deeds to the features on the ground itself. David has frequently stood in the back gardens of properties looking down at the deed plan and then up at the shape of the existing boundary features, and seriously wondered whether or not he was in the right garden.

The practicalities of what actually exists in and around each property must therefore be considered when attempting to apply the deeds to the ground itself.

First of all, let's look again at the deed plan and the dimensions shown on this. As the following examples illustrate, when it comes to dimensions, deed plans should always be viewed with suspicion.

In the first example, shown in figure 2, a fence fell down between Nos 23 and 25. It was allowed to stay down so long that memory and record of its exact position both faded.

When the time came to re-erect it, there was no agreement as to where it should go, and both parties got out their deed plans. The deed plan for No. 25 showed

9

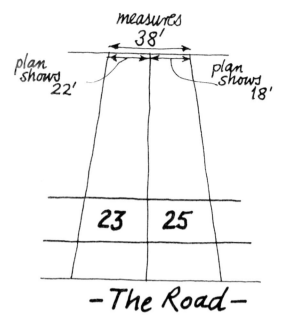

Fig. 2

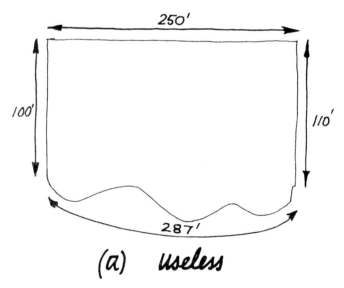

Fig. 3

that the garden was 18 ft wide at the bottom; No. 23's plan indicated a width of 22 ft. Unfortunately, between the fairly rigid fences on the opposite side of the respective gardens, there was only a distance of 38 ft to play with. The more numerate of readers will instantly realise that this leaves us 2 ft short. The very numerate will appreciate that this amounts to about 5% of the whole.

When one is dealing with such narrow back gardens, 2 ft is a lot of width. At least one – and probably both – parties were going to be very unhappy. This is the moment when a surveyor should point out that either the parties should come to a sensible agreement, brokered by the surveyor, or start the legal process. It should be emphasised to the parties that an agreement (over which there is a degree of control) is far preferable to a court judgment (over which there is no control).

A second case headed for a five-day court hearing. The difficulty in this case was that a figured dimension of 287 ft was given against a wavy line. How can you be sure what the waves and kinks are, unless each one is separately dimensioned – and angles or co-ordinates shown as well? A sensible surveyor will refuse even to try to mark that boundary on the ground, but there are those who will, sadly, rely heavily upon it (see figure 3).

It is of no relevance to this point, but worth noting in general, that in the case illustrated in figure 3, no-one was quite sure of the status of the plan, or of who put the figures on it. Nor was the status of the plans certain in the first case (figure 2) described. You should always check your documents for authenticity, and look to see that no unauthorised additions have been made.

With modern surveying instruments, EDM (electromagnetic distance measurement), GPS (global positioning systems) and laser technology, it is now possible to plot all sorts of wonderful shapes and beam them straight into a computer system. While this is ideal for planning new housing estates, suspension bridges, motorways and shopping malls, it should be borne in mind that the original deed plans were probably drawn-up by hand by someone who was using an uncalibrated cloth tape, measuring up a slope. You can't make a silk survey out of a sow's plan.

Indeed, even if you are dealing with what looks like a rectangular plot, and all four dimensions are given, you still can't be absolutely sure that you know where everything should be. If the angles are not right – i.e. 90° – then you could have a rhomboid plot. Alternatively, you could have a rhomboid plan and a right-angled plot. It all depends on whether the draughtsman or the site agent was better at angles.

Sometimes, only the original deed plan will tell the whole truth, so that even the best available copies don't reveal all. The next anecdote illustrates this.

A client owned a house in north London. He purchased the site next door, on which the pair of his semi-detached house had stood, but had been demolished, and later he resold it, retaining his original house. An argument then arose about the ownership of what had – at least at one time – been the wall between the houses. The client was certain that when he sold the vacant plot he had retained the whole wall. The other side were equally sure that they had the right to use it as a party wall for their new building. All the plans produced by the client, copied from the deeds, appeared to be undoctored and seemed to indicate that he was right. But a photocopy is only a photocopy and the original title held by the Land Registry (LR) was examined. When the pie was opened, the bird that began to sing was not serenading the client. The red line clearly ran through the middle of the wall.

Shakespeare said that a 'crooked figure may attest in little place a million'. The thin red line on a deed plan is often several inches thick, and can be a foot or so. Deed plans have their uses, but they also have their limitations. You should certainly not embark on a boundary dispute without seeing what your plans can tell you, but you shouldn't pursue an acrimonious and expensive argument based solely on their evidence.

There's also the question of ownership. Many boundary disputes require an early clarification of who *owns* a particular boundary feature – because many disputes start with a complaint regarding the attachment of objects such as trellises or washing lines to '*my* wall'. Technically, if you own the wall or the fence, you are within your rights in objecting to such affixing. These are the sorts of questions that can often be resolved by reading – and applying – the deeds.

Ownership leads on to maintenance – and an early practical question: whose duty is it, if anyone's, to maintain a particular fence (or wall)? You can sometimes find this out by (once more) referring to the deeds, where there may be some words that will help. You are looking for something like: 'the fence on the eastern boundary is to be maintained by the owner of (your property)', or 'all walls and fences are party walls and fences, jointly maintainable'. If there are no such helpful clauses – or

13

even if there are, and you cannot tell east from butter (as John used to say) – then look at the plan. This may have one or more 'T' marks on it (figure 4).

The 'T' indicates that ownership of a boundary feature lies with the owner within whose land it appears. Therefore, in figure 4, No. 39 owns the fence on his right (as he looks out of his back window) and the one at the bottom of his garden. You can see why 'the eastern boundary' may not be immediately obvious without such a mark. If there is a duty to maintain those features – which will not be apparent without reading the deeds – the 'T' marks will make it clear where that duty lies.

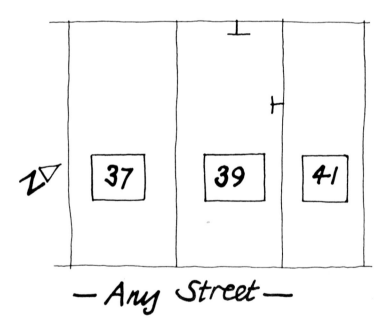

Fig. 4

So what do you do if your neighbour starts to carefully erect a fence which you – not him – are legally responsible to maintain? Well, there are a number of options open to you. If you are happy with its appearance and position, you can, like Brer Fox, lie low and say nothing. If you're on friendly terms with your neighbour, you may wish to offer to contribute to – or even to bear – the cost. If you are confident that the fence is not on your land, and you do not like the look of it, you could put up your own version, face-to-face with your neighbour's, thus fulfilling your legal obligation and giving yourself what you want to look at.

And what if your neighbour, having newly purchased his house and observed a dilapidated fence when viewing the property, asks you politely to maintain the fence? Firstly – and equally politely – check he has got his facts about ownership right. If he has, and you own the fence, then comply.

If you are a freeholder on a newly developed estate, or a leasehold owner, it is much more likely that you will be bound to maintain a fence or wall. However (contrary to what many people think), surprisingly often there is no obligation regarding maintenance at all. You may own a fence, but you do not necessarily have to strive officiously to keep it alive. Nor, contrariwise, may your neighbour have any duty to succour it. Once again, you should be sure of your ground before you start either antagonising the people you have to live next to, or lining the pockets of solicitors and surveyors with your hard-earned money. Mostly, they don't need it.

General and determined boundaries

As discussed in Chapter 1, boundaries shown on Land Registry (LR) title plans are 'general boundaries'.

The general boundary system relies upon property owners being content to look at the features that separate their gardens from those of their neighbours and accept that somewhere within the privet hedge lies the legal boundary. Most people, of course, think exactly that and have no problems whatsoever. Others feel that their boundaries should be defined in some way so that all uncertainty can be removed.

In many parts of the world, particularly in current and former Commonwealth countries, there is what is broadly known as a 'cadastral' system. In essence, this means that boundaries are fixed by angles and distances, very precisely. Corners of properties can be fixed to millimetres by a licensed land surveyor.

In mainland Europe this system is also common; when walking along the streets of most European towns, if one looks down, the little boundary markers where shop frontages join can often be seen.

We, in England and Wales, do not have a cadastral system in place. There are land surveyors, particularly those who have returned from many years of surveying in countries where the cadastral system reigns, who spend the rest of their careers trying to convert everyone they meet to the merits of such a system and the advantages it would bring.

What they forget, of course, is that it would cost millions (possibly billions) of pounds to introduce such a system from scratch and that that money would presumably have to be found by the taxpayer. In the meantime, the general boundary system, in broad terms, works well as it is. If one flies into Heathrow airport and looks out of the window of the aircraft onto suburban London, one can see thousands and thousands of houses – very few of which actually have boundary disputes. The disputes that do flare up are, on the whole, funded by the participants. All in all, it is unlikely that the public funding of a cadastral system would be a vote-winner at any general election.

However, if two adjacent property owners wish to have their boundary fixed (or 'determined', being the correct word), then they can apply to the LR to do so, using Form DB and the new *Land Registration Rules* 2003.

A determined boundary gives a result as good as any cadastral system – probably better – but is confined to the length of boundary between those two consenting neighbours. Form DB must be accompanied by a large-scale plan (typically 1:200 scale), with precise measurements (to 10 mm accuracy, or half an inch), before it will be accepted by the LR. The LR publishes guidelines on its website, www.landreg.org, which may change from time to time as methods and surveying equipment advance. The measurements are carried out by privately instructed land surveyors (not LR staff) and submitted to the LR for approval. The cost of the process is thus dictated by the cost of the on-site surveying.

It cannot be stressed too often how much cheaper it is – not to mention making for better relations while you continue to live next to each other – to approach your neighbour in a spirit of friendly co-operation in jointly determining any point where there may be doubt. You are much more likely to achieve an amicable settlement by saying, 'Since the fence fell down, I can't really tell where the boundary is. Can you remember where it ought to be?' than by simply putting the fence back up where you think it ought to be, even if you get it right. It is invariably well worth giving up an inch or two of garden in most cases for the sake of neighbourly relations and peace of mind – and much, much less expensive than fighting about it, especially in court.

This is, of course, general advice on personal relations, rather than boundary disputes – but when a boundary dispute threatens, do try to see your neighbour face-to-face if you want to discuss anything, rather than just writing a letter. Unfortunately, even this is not an infallible method of settling disputes: many clients report that they took the plans in next door or invited their neighbours in for a cup of coffee and everything seemed friendly and agreed, but as soon as the workmen started to put the fence up, the neighbours became incensed and called the police. Sometimes both sides tell much the same story and allege all sorts of villainy by the other. Human nature is very difficult. You can but try.

Housing estates and developers' layout plans

As we advance further into the 21st century, there seems to be an ever greater need for housing. Much of this need is being satisfied by the building of huge new housing estates on what is known as greenfield land.

There are hidden dangers in the process of starting with a green field and ending up with 120 houses. These dangers can lead to unnecessary boundary disputes, purely out of ignorance of the way in which the houses came to be where they are in the first place.

The following example is given in great detail, but no apologies are made for this, because the process of building a new housing estate should be understood by all those who live on one and have boundary problems.

First of all there is the greenfield site: probably several fields, probably not very green, and including overgrown hedges, muddy watercourses and brambles. Into this terrain steps the chartered land surveyor, armed with a vast array of electronic wizardry. Avoiding the perils of broken ankles and severed arteries, a precise map is made.

On a typical site for 120 houses, there will be something like 10,000 survey readings (angles, distances, levels, feature-codes, and so on) all going into the surveyor's computer's brain. A red and white pole will be held upright but, every now and again, the poleholder will sneeze or let concentration drift and that particular measurement won't be quite as accurate as it should be. It should also be expected (although not accepted) that the odd reading in every 1,000 will be wrong. The result is a map that would make surveyors of the good old days of the 1950s and 1960s green with envy, produced in a matter of days, but with some flaws (although not as many flaws as in the 'good old days')!

In the good old days, architects would also have some surveying knowledge and would probably take check-levels on site and have a poke around to look at the hedges, and so on. Now, thankfully, architects tend to leave all that to the land surveyor (professional indemnity insurance companies have put paid to dabbling in other people's disciplines) and the land surveyor's high-tech map is taken as being 100% correct (as it should be, in an ideal world) by the architect. The high-tech process employed to reach this stage also convinces the conveyancers that the layout plan can be used for paper-title purposes.

The map for the estate is produced by a system known as CAD (computer-aided design), in the form of a computer file with layers of detail that can be switched on and off. Sometimes, vital layers are accidentally left switched-off by the architect and so design errors can occur. For example, it is not unknown for a road to be designed 'on-screen' that goes straight through a protected tree. In other cases, a road can be designed that avoids the protected tree on the land surveyor's map, but where that tree has been plotted in the wrong place by the land surveyor. When the road is pegged-out, it once again goes straight through the tree!

Let's say that the architect and surveyor are blissfully unaware of all this and the estate is designed and full planning permission is obtained. The plan (with all the houses, roads, manholes, etc.) is known as the 'layout plan'. The developer awards the groundworks contract to the firm with the cheapest price, and the machines, portakabins and men with shovels arrive on site. This is when things start going wrong. Not by a lot, but by enough to bring the subject back to boundary disputes.

The problem of roads going through trees will be discovered fairly quickly. Let's take another example, in which we will assume that the land surveyor's map and the layout plan are perfect. On this particular site, amid the mud and apparent chaos, a setting-out engineer pegs out the main drainage run. A few hours later, a dumper truck driver accidentally reverses over one of the pegs and, blessed with a diligent nature, gets down from his truck and places the peg back where it came from. The problem is that he places the peg back where he *thinks* it came from, which happens to be 1.5 metres away from where it actually should be – and off he drives. The drainage pipes go in (nobody is aware that one of the manholes is in the wrong place) and then the roads are pegged out. Calamity! The main drainage must run beneath the road (not under houses or through front gardens) and yet the road appears to miss one of the manholes by 1.5 metres. Nobody knows why. Nasty letters are sent back and forth between developer, architect and surveyor, all putting their umbrellas up, while, in complete innocence, the dumper truck driver continues to drive around the site with a merry countenance.

What happens? Well, to prevent a long story becoming even longer, the road is tweaked so that the errant manhole is within its width. This means that the houses also have to be tweaked, so that the front drives are of the correct minimum length. Then the fencing contractor comes along and erects the garden fences – perfectly sensibly, by reference to the houses (and not to the global position shown on the layout plan).

The estate is now completed and everything looks fine. Anyone glancing at the layout plan and looking at the beautifully landscaped mock-Tudor estate will assume that they are one and the same. They are not. If an as-built survey is carried out (and some diligent developers do this), then all the differences will be seen by placing this over the layout plan on a light table. It is a general rule that rarely do the two match. Usually, there are angular swings all over the estate, as problems have been overcome, house-types changed, pegs knocked over, and countless other things adjusted.

Then the only thing waiting to be thrown into the melting pot is, say, a retired maths teacher moving into one of the houses and his neighbour being a family with several exuberant teenage children. Trouble soon flares up (noise, perceived insolence, etc.) and the maths teacher buys a scale rule and starts examining his deeds (i.e. the red line marking his boundary on what is a photocopy of the layout plan). The reader's time need not be taken up with what happens next.

In summary, all that can be said is that a good boundary surveyor should be able to explain all of the above to a client who has a boundary dispute involving a housing estate property and should also be able to point out that if all the boundaries on the estate were to be put right, it would be necessary to demolish the whole estate and start all over again. These sorts of disputes can generate tens of thousands of pounds in legal fees (and there isn't really an answer other than 'you bought what you saw, and you saw what you bought').

If the surveyor is unable to prevent intransigence in such cases, then mediation is a much better answer than going to the local county court.

# Adverse possession

Strange as it may seem to those who don't know these things, you can acquire someone else's land simply by taking very solid possession of it. If one of these walls or fences – the correct position of which we are making such a fuss about in this book – has been in the 'wrong' place for a certain number of years, then, in a process known as 'adverse possession', that can become the 'right' place, as the 'wrong' person becomes its 'rightful' owner.

Of course, deliberately to encroach upon someone else's land, and fence or 'wall' it off and use it as your own, is theft, so it would be wrong to encourage those who try to prove adverse possession against the rightful owner. You have to know the legal position, though, in order to protect your own land against adverse possession by an acquisitive neighbour – and also to know when it is probably not worth attempting to reclaim what was once yours.

The legal position varies between unregistered and registered land. Most properties are now registered, and the recent *Land Registration Act* 2002 gives further protection to title-holders against potential adverse possessors. The points noted below apply to registered land under the Act.

There are certain requirements that have to be pretty firmly satisfied to effect adverse possession under the 2002 Act. First of all, there is the fact that you must adversely possess the land in question for at least 12 years before you will be recognised as its rightful owner. The 12 years is really the sum of ten or more years of occupation, plus two for the official action that commences when you attempt to claim adverse possession. If, before the ten years is up, you acknowledge to the rightful owner that you are squatting, the clock will start to run again from the date of that acknowledgement.

Following the introduction of the 2002 Act, a prospective possessor must now be an adjacent owner. This means that it is not possible for someone from Penzance to fence off and then possess a bit of land in Northumberland. The land must adjoin a property that you already own. The class of ownership you will get (of the possessed land, if successful) will be the same as that for the existing land for which you are registered (freehold, leasehold, etc.).

What's more, your occupation and use of the land you have stolen must be in such a manner as obviously to enjoy it for your own purposes, and to debar the rightful owner from his intended use.

It's virtually essential that any land that is claimed is enclosed with a sound wall or fence. Simply to cultivate the land would be very unlikely to be enough to establish adverse possession. Indeed, in one case (*Dear v Woods*, 1984), the asphalting of part of a front drive and even fencing it was held not to be enough to exclude the next-door neighbours from ownership of the disputed area.

It's harder still to get adverse possession against the Crown: there, it takes 30 years. There are other cases, too, where the time will be extended, such as if the owner was under a legal disability when the right of action first arose. Even in those deserving cases, though, time runs out after 30 years.

Let's look in detail at how you might effect – and prevent – adverse possession of a piece of registered land under the 2002 Act. Let us say that Owner A has been in possession of a bit of neighbouring Owner B's property for at least ten years. Owner A can apply to the Land Registry (LR) for adverse possession, preferably with a plan attached to Form ADV1. If the LR is happy that Owner A fulfils the criteria, it will give notice to Owner B, saying, in effect, 'you have two years to do something about the presence of Owner A on your property'. If, as will be the most common outcome, Owner B takes legal action to evict Owner A from the occupied land within two years, then Owner B will win. If, however, Owner B does nothing and lets the two years drift by, then Owner A will automatically be given title to the possessed land.

It appears, following the enactment of the 2002 Act, that adverse possession of registered property will become very rare indeed. However, the Act still underlines the importance of keeping the LR fully informed of your whereabouts if you are an absentee owner of land. Three contact addresses can be lodged at the LR, including an electronic address, so if you own registered land somewhere in England and Wales, and embark on a two-year tour of Australia, it's worth popping into the nearest internet café every now and again to see if the LR has tried to contact you regarding a potential adverse possessor.

Property owners should always be vigilant. The two most expensive purchases people are likely to make in their lifetimes are their homes and their cars. While people clean the family car every week and note the slightest scratch on the side after parking at the out-of-town shopping mall, they rarely operate the same level of vigilance when maintaining their property limits. The people who spend hours rubbing polish into their car bonnets are often the very same people who do not peer into the bottom, heavily overgrown, corners of their gardens for years on end.

Property owners should regularly check their property boundaries. Where possible, they should also take annual photographs of outer walls, so that any changes from year to year can be spotted before a neighbour can make an ownership claim.

A recent case of owners not noticing what was happening with regard to their property occurred in respect of a party wall. *Prudential Assurance Co Ltd v Waterloo Real Estate Inc* 1999, a case now commonly referred to as *The Great Wall of Knightsbridge*, concerned a length of party wall about 22 ft long and 15 ft high. The Court of Appeal found that the defendants had acquired ownership of the next door's half of the party wall, because among other things, they (or their predecessors) had repaired and decorated the wall, removed graffiti, put up external lighting, cut an opening through the wall and installed a night safe. The 'real' owners had remained oblivious to this.

Aerial photographs

When investigating a boundary dispute, an oft overlooked area is that of aerial photography. Aerial photographs come in two types, oblique and vertical.

Oblique photographs are useful for having a general look at a property. These photographs are usually taken at low altitude by members of the local flying club, clocking-up hours, or by one of the many firms that sell the photographs as framed prints by knocking on front doors. The problem with these photographs is that they are taken at an oblique angle (as the name suggests) and so the relationship between features will appear distorted.

Vertical photographs are much better for helping with boundary disputes and are particularly useful in cases of disputed rights of way and adverse possession. These photographs are usually taken by the Ordnance Survey (OS) or by private aerial survey companies in the business of mapping large swathes of the country for new roads, pipelines, and so on. The photographs are taken at high altitude and the centre of the photograph is exactly below the camera at the moment it goes 'click'. In other words, in mathematical terms, if an imaginary plumbline could be dropped from the camera at the precise moment of the 'click', it would hit the ground at the tangent to the earth's surface, and that would also be the centre of the

28

photograph. These photographs are taken at timed intervals with the aircraft flying in a dead straight line, so that each photograph overlaps the next one (and the preceding one) by 60%. Each overlapping pair of photographs is known as a 'stereo-pair' and the 60% overlap can be viewed in three dimensions using a small hand-held stereoscope.

If more expensive photogrammetric equipment is used, the area can be mapped in great detail. However, it is the use of stereoscope that is most common. In the hands of an experienced user trained in the interpretation of texture, shade and feature identification, it is quite amazing how much detail can be obtained. Individual fence posts can be seen, and walls with or without buttresses, tracks across fields and gates are all visible (gates are not shown on OS maps, incidentally). Obviously, such photographs can be vital when one is trying to prove or disprove adverse possession.

Vertical photographs can be ordered by selecting them from dated flight-plans obtainable from your nearest OS agent; all you need to know is the OS four-figure grid reference and the era of photography you are interested in. Such photographs are widely available from about 1946 onwards.

How large is too little?

De minimis non curat lex. The law does not concern itself with trifles. How large, therefore, does a disputed area of land have to be before the courts will be prepared to order rectification of a boundary? This question is very similar to that asked (and answered) in another of John's books, *Anstey's Rights of Light,* as to what is meant by 'small'. The best legal opinion obtained on that – and it might apply equally well here – is that it would not be 'large'.

It is always very difficult to get the courts to lay down hard and fast rules – which are of course easier for practitioners to use in advising clients, and ever so much easier for lay people to understand. If you were able to say (as an adviser) to your client, 'The courts have held that to move a suburban back garden boundary 2 inches is *de minimis,* but to move it 3 inches is actionable', life would be straightforward. However, even when surveyors had a nice simple rule to follow in rights of light cases (the 50/50 rule, which said that if 50% of a room remained well lit, it hadn't been injured), the courts soon returned them to a state of indecision by saying that it wasn't to be relied on for certain. Very jealous of their prerogatives, the courts.

One case in which John Anstey was instructed involved two neighbours, each of whom had, over the years, alleged various misdeeds on the part of the other (unrelated to boundaries). When John's client, one of the neighbours, renewed the fence between their respective back gardens, there was bound to be trouble.

John was instructed through solicitors in the dispute and carefully surveyed the scene of the crime. He produced a plan (figure 5), which showed that the greatest distance the fence had strayed from the straight and narrow (the back gardens were approximately 30 ft wide) was 7 inches. 'Marvellous,' said the solicitors, 'that's *de minimis*.'

The other side's expert gave his evidence; John gave his evidence; the judge gave his decision: 'I accept Mr Anstey's evidence entirely, and find for the other side.' In his opinion, 7 inches was not *de minimis* in suburban back gardens.

With the courts extremely reluctant to lay down rigidly fixed guidelines, this decision does not, unfortunately, give you licence to assert that a tapering movement of 7 inches, or the wrongful enclosure of about 8 sq. ft, will always be actionable. Still less does it allow you to assert that any smaller change would not be corrected by the courts. It is a question of fact, degree and proportionality in each case – but at least this decision gives you a useful pointer.

The best help that can be given in the opposite direction comes from a case that involved a party wall – or not, as the boundary might be. In this instance, if the wall was astride the boundary, then it was a party wall under the

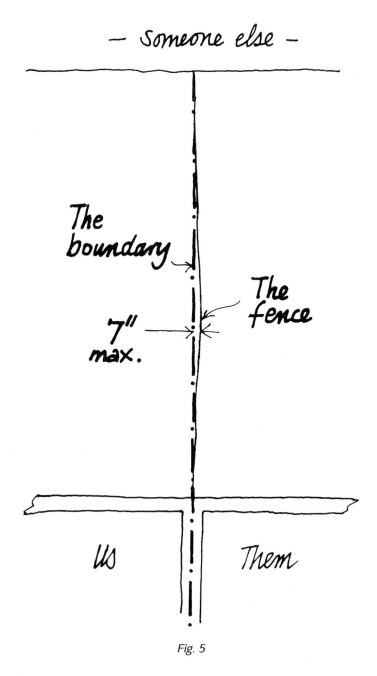

Fig. 5

London Building Acts (this was before the *Party Wall etc. Act* 1996 came into being) and those who were seeking to raise on it (Party A) would have to serve notice. If it was wholly on their land, they could do what they liked.

The strong point in favour of Party A was that the wall and their building appeared to have been built at the same time in the same bricks. A point in Party B's favour was that the history of the two sites strongly indicated that they weren't, in fact, built contemporaneously. There were one or two well-fixed points lying about, and some pretty exactly stated measurements in sales particulars, conveyances, and the like. Starting from one of the best fixed points and measuring to the wall, the result was, if the measurements on the plans were accurate, that the 9-inch wall was 1.5 inches on one side and 7.5 inches on the other side of the boundary. (This would be quite enough to make it a party wall by definition.) The evidence was not seriously challenged on facts or disturbed in cross-examination, but the judge found that 'none of the measurements was exact enough to be relied upon for the position of the boundary', and therefore depended on the visual evidence of the consanguinity as proof that the wall belonged to the owners of the building. This case is a hint – no more – that 1.5 inches (38 mm) is *de minimis*.

But for goodness sake. When you consider how accurate your measurements are likely to be, then however sophisticated your equipment (and this isn't a book about advanced surveying techniques, because you rarely have a starting point reliable enough to justify their use in the sort of situations being described), then two inches or so are surely just not worth worrying about.

If there is any question of the matter falling under this head, there are even more grounds than usual for ramming down the unwilling client's throat the desirability of forgetting about the whole thing, or else reaching a settlement with his neighbour, however much he detests him.

On the subject of numbers, readers will have noted that this book darts around between metric and imperial measurements. Most surveyors fall into one of two camps. There are the modernists who favour the metric system (which is, in any case, the lawful system in many parts of our lives today) and the traditionalists who favour the old imperial system of feet and inches. Anyone who has studied paper-title documents will agree that nearly every one has dimensions in feet and inches and it would be a sign of arrogance for the surveyor to convert them all into metres. If a property frontage is shown on the deeds as being 60 ft, then it would be silly to keep referring to that frontage as 18.288 metres; all that would be achieved would be confusion all round. The best way to satisfy the modernist *and* the traditionalist – and more importantly the trial judge – is to show both, with one in brackets: 60 ft (18.288 metres) or 20 metres (65 ft 7 inches). This sensible rule is even followed in places in this book.

Incidentally, an eminent land surveyor recently said that a mixture of the two systems would be ideal. He would like a system that used metres for large measurements, feet for medium-sized measurements, inches for small measurements and millimetres for tiny measurements. The mind boggles at the thought of a dimension of 45 metres, 8 ft, 6 in, 3 mm, but it shows that lateral thinking still exists!

Party walls and 'party' walls

Between walls inside and outside London there used to be a great gulf fixed.

Party walls inside London used to be governed by the *London Building Acts*, especially the *Amendment Act* of 1939, while everywhere else in England and Wales (Scotland is always different), common law ruled. In 1996, a public-spirited group of surveyors succeeded in getting the *Party Wall etc. Act* through Parliament. The Act came into full force in September 1997, and now the whole of England and Wales shares the benefits that were formerly those of London alone. The Act grants extraordinary powers to an owner of one half of a wall to treat the other half of it almost as if it were his own. On the other hand, that owner cannot treat *his* half as if it were his own, without taking his neighbour into his confidence and, in effect, discussing with him how it should be dealt with. Rather than go on at length, readers should simply refer to *Anstey's Party Walls* (another book in this series) for more information.

The importance of this chapter to this book is that in dealing with party walls in England and Wales, precise boundaries are not always relevant to what you can or cannot do to a wall. In Scotland – and Northern Ireland for the time being – they may still be.

In the first edition of this book, there was an elegant joke about the right to access a neighbour's land being comparable to the snakes in Ireland. This is no longer true, though it might as well be for all the use that the *Access to Neighbouring Land Act* 1992 is proving in providing the help it was meant to. (For a full explanation of this Act, see the RICS Soundtrack/Owlion tape of the same name, available from RICS Books.) Unfortunately, the operation of the 1992 Act depends on the courts (unlike the *Party Wall etc. Act*, which is managed by surveyors) and is so unwieldy that the words 'sledgehammer' and 'nut' spring to mind.

Briefly, the 1992 Act says that if you have asked permission to go on to your neighbour's land, and have been refused, you may seek consent from the courts. Access will only be granted for maintenance or repair, not for new building, and may be subject to strict conditions as to time and other matters. In addition, in non-domestic cases you will have to pay handsomely for the privilege. Apart from the use of this Act, there is a rather tenuous right to go on to your neighbour's property to restore support to your own, if your neighbour is allowing his property to decay.

With this in mind, the correct position of a boundary is of considerable importance. And whereas a few feet or even yards may not matter on a moor, a few inches can be of critical importance between suburban houses. The business of resolving disputes on such issues is probably one of the most expensive ways of passing the time that can be found.

The most common cause of disputes about the position of the boundary in a party wall is eccentricity – not on the part of the owners, although there's quite a bit of that flying about – but in the walls. If the wall is symmetrical, then, as in the case of garden walls (which we discuss in Chapter 16), you can fairly safely assume that the boundary runs down the middle. The trouble comes when the wall is shaped like the one in the illustration below (figure 6).

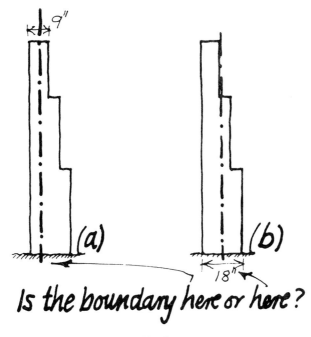

Is the boundary here or here?

Fig. 6

The question then arises: was the wall built like this, astride the boundary, or was it built as a straightforward 9-inch (say) wall, which one owner has since thickened for his own purposes? The answer may depend on which parts of the wall are older, if you can tell. Look at the next illustration (figure 7).

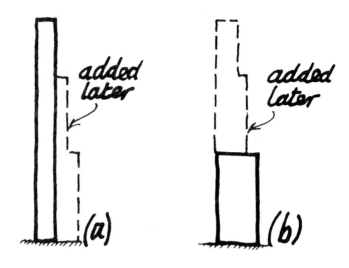

Fig. 7

If the original wall appears to be as shown in figure 7(a), 9 inches from top to bottom, with thicknessing added by one owner on one side, presumably in order to take his new, heavier structure, you can be fairly sure that the boundary is as shown in figure 6(a), i.e., in the centre of the 9-inch chunk. If, on the other hand, the wall seems originally to have been lower, perhaps only two storeys high, and one owner has raised it, getting the maximum area for his new upper floors by setting his raised portion as far over as possible, as shown in figure 7(b), then the boundary will be as shown in figure 6(b), in the centre of the original 18-inch structure.

Now that the *Party Wall etc. Act* rules, it is also important to know whether a wall has been thickened or whether it is two separate skins. If the former, then the whole wall may be a party wall, albeit eccentrically astride the boundary; if the latter, it is quite probable that each party owns one skin, and the boundary runs between them.

If you can't tell what the history of a wall is, and you are forced to guess, the best option is to plump for figure 6(a) – but that assumes that there is nothing to point you towards another or a better-founded answer. Always prefer evidence to guesses.

The boundary between attached houses

An attached house can either be part of a terrace (figure 8) or one of a pair of semi-detached properties (figure 9). In the context of this book, its most important feature is that it shares at least one wall with a neighbour.

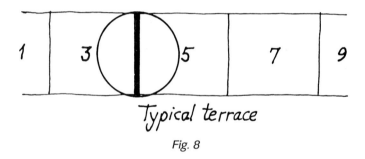

Typical terrace

Fig. 8

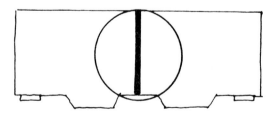

Typical pair of semi d's.

Fig. 9

In the absence of clear proof to the contrary, such as an unequivocal statement in a deed, or a plan in which the boundary is distinctly shown to include the whole of the wall within one party's ownership, as in figure 10, the dividing line between the properties can be assumed to be the centre line of the common (or 'party') wall, as shown in figure 11.

Sometimes, perhaps even usually, this sort of boundary causes absolutely no problem at all. The wall is quite straightforward, as shown in figure 11, and each party's ownership of, and rights in, their own half are clear.

Complications can exist, even in this simple form of dividing wall, but they tend to be complications more of use than of ownership. One such is when the builder has skimped on the brickwork and intermingled the flues, or at least only just kept the flues on their own side of the boundary (figures 12 and 13).

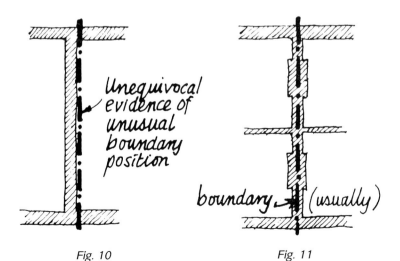

Unequivocal evidence of unusual boundary position

boundary (usually)

Fig. 10   Fig. 11

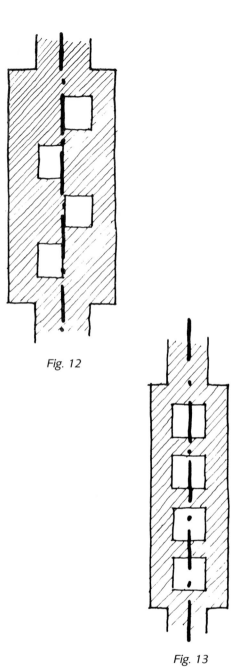

Fig. 12

Fig. 13

Fortunately, the sort of flue illustrated in figure 13 is comparatively rare. When it occurs, however, it has been known to cause confusion as to the position of the boundary. The chap who is doing some work to the chimney breast in his property opens up the flues, and concludes that his ownership must extend at least as far as the back of the flues, and possibly half a brick beyond. This is probably not so – although there are no known leading cases on the subject – but it is suggested that each party has an easement to have his smoke or fumes pass up the flue within his neighbour's property. Should one party choose to rebuild without a chimney, he would have a right to do so only up to the centre-line. In so doing he would, naturally, also have to respect next-door's cross-easement in their flues. It has been known for this unhappy arrangement only to be made apparent when next-door's live flue spouts smoke into the neighbour's fire-less house.

The alternative interpretation of the boundary in these circumstances is that it should run in zigzag fashion around the flues. In the absence of documentary evidence, this seems to be an unlikely hypothesis.

This chapter will conclude by restating the norm. Usually, the boundary line between buildings with a common wall runs down the centre of that wall.

The 'L'-shaped house

One of the most common layouts of housing which gives rise to doubt about the position of the boundary is the street full of L-shaped houses (figure 14).

To many people, it is obvious that as the wall of the rear extension forms part of their building, and only bounds the garden of next-door, the wall must belong wholly to them. They are almost always wrong. As the wall between the two gardens usually abuts the rear

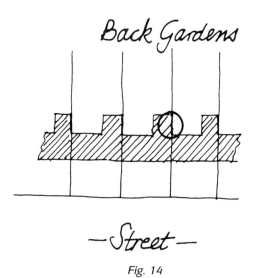

Fig. 14

projection, and forms a continuation of the wall of the house, the error as to ownership of the house wall is frequently extended in similar fashion to produce a mistake about the garden wall as well.

Unfortunately, this readily understandable confusion can give rise to a lot of ill-feeling between neighbours. Show the following illustration (figure 15) to any doubters, and perhaps they will understand.

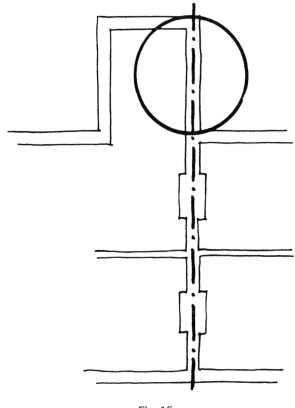

Fig. 15

In the vast majority of cases, the wall of the rear
extension is a continuation of the wall between the main
parts of the houses. As we have seen in an earlier chapter,
it is usually safe to assume that the boundary between the
houses is the centre line of the dividing wall. Unless the
deed plan shows a definite kink – and that is an
extremely rare occurrence – the boundary can equally
safely be assumed to continue in a straight line. Half the
rear extension wall, therefore, sits on the land of the
adjoining owner.

It is, of course, essential to check that both the
assumptions just described are in fact correct. Look at the
deeds to make sure that you are not dealing with a rare
occurrence in which the boundary does jink to one side,
and take measurements to prove that the rear wall is a
continuation of the main one – or isn't, for that matter.
If the deeds are straightforward – or, at any rate,
straight – and the wall is likewise, then QED: the wall is
a 'party' one.

Streets

It has been said that there are two kinds of people in the world: those who divide things into two categories, and those who don't. It has also been said that there are three types of surveyor in the world: those who can count and those who can't.

One of the distinctions drawn in a previous chapter of this book was between walls formerly inside the jurisdiction of the *London Building Acts* and those outside. In this chapter, a similar but more restrictive distinction may be made: between those streets inside the City of London and those outside.

Outside the City, the doctrine of '*ad medium filum*' – to which the word '*viae*' is sometimes added – usually applies. That means that if you own land fronting on to a highway, you are deemed to own up to the middle of the street, even if this is not shown on the deed plan or mentioned in the conveyance. While the road continues to function, the highway authority owns as much of the surface and topsoil (if that's the right word) of the land as is necessary for its statutory operations, and the public has all its customary rights to pass along the road.

When a road is closed, however, and the rights are extinguished for some reason (perhaps a new road has been built, making the old road redundant), the ownership reverts to the frontage. The word 'reverts' is used because the assumption that justifies allowing the owner to take possession of half the road width is that he gave it up in the first place – or his primordial ancestor did – in order to allow the road to be formed. If you can get a road stopped up, you can therefore add enormously to your plot and thence to any potential development.

When using front-to-back dimensions on a deed plan, it is worth checking that they do commence at the current front of the property, as it is not unknown for the front end of such a measurement to start in the middle of the road. A dispute in Hull some years ago hinged upon two surveyors' differing interpretations of where the middle of a road used to be before it was adopted by the council, as that was the starting point for the measurements. The matter was not helped by the fact that the rear end of the same dimension line was shown as being the edge of a canal bank, but did not say whether it was the top or bottom of the bank (the difference between which was about the same as the difference between the surveyors' interpretation of the road centre line).

The practice of *ad medium filum* derives from legal presumption, and is not an invariable rule. Actual facts may displace the presumption, such as the outright sale of the road to the local authority. The existence of vaults under the street, on the other hand, will strongly support a claim to the ownership beneath the road.

Vaults may be relevant in connection with the second of our two categories: streets inside the City of London (and incidentally in Dorking, where underground caves follow a pattern that bears little relationship to what goes on

above ground). Most of the streets in the City of London
are chartered, and the City owns them hook, line and
sinker; or, to put it another way, *usque ad coelum et ad
inferos*. The frontager does not then own *ad medium
filum*.

Despite the City's ownership of the street, one can still
own the vaults under the street. The author Trevor
Aldridge (to whose book on *Boundaries, Walls and
Fences* John gratefully nodded, in telling the following
story) relates that his firm's premises had lavatories in the
vaults beneath a City street. When some doubt arose as
to ownership of the vaults, the firm's then senior partner
made a statutory declaration that he had used the WCs,
man and boy, for the past X years, and that the firm had
thus acquired a squatter's (sic) title to them.

Overhanging and underpinning

In London – that is to say, the part of it that was covered by the *London Building Acts* – it is usually fairly safe to assume that the face of the external wall of a building forms the boundary, rather than any imaginary line formed by projecting downwards from the eaves or upward from the foundations. The reason for this is that the *London Buildings Act (Amendment) Act* 1939, and then the *Party Wall etc. Act* 1996, specifically gave a right to cut off any projections of that sort, when it was necessary to do so in order for a building owner to erect his own wall on the boundary. This seems to assume (and it cannot be overstressed how dangerous assumptions are) that a man will get the maximum enclosure for his building that he can, and hope to get away for as long as possible with the additional projections.

Although section 6 of the *Party Wall etc. Act* 1996 states that the Act does not 'authorise any interference with any easement...relating to a party wall', it can be argued that not only do the express provisions of section 2(2)(h) (which deals with cutting off projections) override the generality of the later section, but also that such projections are usually attached to an independent wall, rather than a party one.

The right to cut off projections would also seem to exclude by implication the possibility that adverse possession (see the eponymous chapter) might be claimed in respect of land between footings and eaves. You'd have to do something far more exclusive to make such a presumption stick. In other words, the mere ownership of elements above and below someone else's land will not give you any chance of claiming the space between.

It is quite clear at common law that when you sell a building with such projecting features, the whole of the building passes from vendor to purchaser, even if the land is correctly described and shown as being limited to the face of the wall. This is expressly confirmed by *Truckell v Stock* (1957). The air space between the projections remains in the ownership of next door and, following the *Party Wall etc. Act*, you can no longer acquire an easement to have your eaves and foundations projecting into next-door's land, without the fear of losing (see figure 16).

There was a dispute next door to a church in Hampstead, where an adjoining owner dug up an obscure case to prove – as he thought – that he did own the land above his projecting footings. No amount of argument or exposition of the law would persuade him otherwise. In the end, the church was advised to carry on building up to what it was convinced was the boundary (the face of his wall) and see whether he was prepared to put his money where his mouth was. He wasn't.

Overhanging trees present a different sort of problem. The law as to responsibility for a tree's actions is quite straightforward. Whoever planted it stops the buck – or his successor in title does. Very often, the roots and

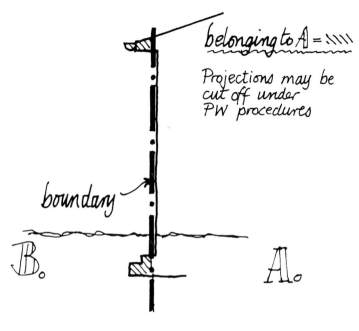

Fig. 16

branches of a tree will bridge the boundary, and sometimes even its trunk does. Since, as every schoolboy used to know, 'great oaks from little acorns grow', a sapling planted clearly on one side of an infinitely thin line can easily grow into a tree straddling that line, with a substantial amount of wood on each side of it.

In one typical case, which started out as a 'damage' case, and then turned into a boundary one, Owner A's house was somewhere on the north side of London, and had belonged to a famous wartime Air Vice-Marshal, or some such. The house next door was complaining that its west wing – to put it rather too grandly: it was really the kitchen extension, with a bedroom over it – was being attacked by the roots of Owner A's giant oak tree. There was no doubt about the damage, and very little about the cause of it; the bill was going to be substantial.

In the course of discussions between John Anstey (the surveyor) and Owner A, it emerged that the neighbours had proposed to chop down the tree, and John's client had refused to allow them to do so, claiming the tree as his own. When John asked why it had been necessary to 'claim' it, he was told that the boundaries were very uncertain in that area: there was a public footpath between 'our' grounds and 'their' garden. Careful examination of the deeds and the local council's plans revealed that, although parts of the tree were certainly within the client's land, it could well be argued that the seed had originally fallen outside.

John advised him to put this forward. 'But I love that tree', he protested, 'and they might chop it down'. 'Which', John asked, 'would you prefer: losing the tree or paying the damages?' He disclaimed the tree, the action for damages was withdrawn, and John sent in his bill based, as always, on time expended, with nothing extra for the ingenuity he had displayed on behalf of his client. John noted in an earlier edition of this book that it will probably come as no surprise to those of you versed in the ingratitude of clients that this client refused to pay John's bill in full, supported by his solicitor, because he could not see how he had spent so much time on the job. John had, of course, spent a lot of time on the claim before he discovered that there might be a cheaper way out for his client: much cheaper, since he bilked John as well.

If overhanging branches or projecting roots cause offence to a neighbour, that neighbour can lop them off, so long as he offers anything cut off back to the owner (most people, when offered their branches will politely – or impolitely – decline). Like Shylock, however, the neighbour must be careful not to cut one iota beyond the permitted limits.

This may not be as easy to avoid as it sounds. David has known a case where a person cut back the overhanging branches of his neighbour's tree, taking great care to avoid cutting even one inch over the boundary. To his dismay, the tree, having had the weight of the branches removed, then sprang back, so that it appeared that he had cut beyond the boundary. Much arguing with his neighbour followed, and David was not able to resolve the problem (which subsequently settled into a mutual stand-off between the neighbours).

A property owner can also, in appropriate cases, seek an injunction to restrain the offending objects from growing. As trees are notorious for failing to observe the dictates of the court, their owners will have to comply on their behalf.

A tree preservation order (TPO) applies to a whole tree, so an adjoining owner cannot use self-help on any part of a protected tree. It is not certain where that leaves the adjoining owner if the roots are causing damage (although this does not matter for the purpose of this book). A friendly barrister has given an off-the-cuff opinion that your only recourse against an offending tree protected by a TPO would be to apply to the local authority for removal of the order, or at least a variation sufficient to let you abate the damage-causing elements.

What you do if they refuse, and whether an action would lie against the council, even the barrister wasn't sure, but you could probably apply for judicial review of the council's decision.

The word 'underpinning' was only included in the title of this chapter for euphony's sake, but perhaps it can usefully be added that before the passing of the *Party Wall etc. Act*, a person had no right to underpin beyond the exact boundary of his property, which made dealing with a 'party' wall distinctly difficult, if there was an unco-operative neighbour. Nowadays, in England and Wales, you can underpin the whole wall, but you can't put reinforcement on the far side of the boundary unless your neighbour agrees.

Horizontal boundaries

There is a general presumption in English law that *cuius est solus eius est usque ad coelum et ad inferos*. This may be roughly translated as meaning that if you own the land, you own everything under it and over it.

There are, however, many instances, particularly in the commercial sectors of major cities, where boundaries are three-dimensional: that is they are vertical (as normal and as discussed throughout this book), and also horizontal – they have lower and upper limits, rather like a small pile of cubes of sugar. Obviously, properties cannot sit directly on top of each other like cubes of sugar, as there is usually a gap between the ceiling of one property and the floorboards of the one above. This gap may contain air-conditioning ducts for the lower property, electrical wires for the upper property and telecom cables for both properties. There will almost certainly be joists and other fixings in wooden floors and service flues in concrete floors.

The following anecdote, concerning a redevelopment that certain property magnates were wanting to carry out, illustrates the effects of horizontal boundaries.

The magnates owned a five-storey building, let out in many small tenancies. They had succeeded in buying out all the tenants except one, who held a ground floor shop together with its small back yard. The new building was intended to be deeper than the old (i.e. to measure more from front to back), and the magnates therefore proposed to preserve the single obstinate tenant in place, while they constructed their new office block over, round, and behind him. They were deeply distressed to be told that they could not develop over the shop's back yard because, no vertical limitation having been placed on the demise, all the air space above the yard had also been let to the tenant. They could have coped with the shop, but not with the yard as well, so that removal of the tenant became essential, instead of just highly desirable. Fortunately, the party wall surveyor (a certain J Anstey!) was able to persuade the tenant of the advantages of moving.

There have been one or two cases in the courts where this failure to limit a demise vertically has led to disputes as to the ownership of roof space. In a case studied in the preparation of this book, a failure by a landlord specifically to limit a tenancy to a particular point above a flat, such as the top of the ceiling joists, led to a finding by the court that the tenants were entitled to use the space in the roof above their ceiling for storage.

A second case was brought in the late 1980s. In this case, the demise of a top flat included the top surface of the ceiling to a lower flat, and the roof. It was held that there was an implication that the airspace above the flat had been demised, and that therefore the tenant was entitled to raise the roof and convert the loft to provide additional living space.

As a result of these cases, it can almost certainly safely be said that the legal position of the top element in any structure is fairly straightforward – insofar as one can ever be sure that anything is definite in the law (where, it often seems, the quixotic decisions of the courts are far more likely to vary than the advice given by a competent surveyor). Unless an upper limit is specifically set by a legal document, the owner owns, or the tenant leases, everything upwards from his holding.

The situation is far less clear when you have an upper and a lower hereditament. It has been held that the demise of a flat must extend upwards at least as far as the underside of the joists to which the ceiling is attached, but no similar decision has been found in a downwards direction. Logic suggests that the top of the joists to which the floorboards are fixed must be the minimum extent to which an upper flat will read downwards.

In addition, no decision has been found regarding ownership of, or responsibility for, the joists between the upper and the nether millstone. It might be reasonable to assume that, in the absence of specific words to the contrary, each party would own up to (or down to) half-way; but it would probably be safer to assume that if you made any such presumption the courts would upset it.

The lesson to be learnt – and which indeed seems to be being learnt by modern-day lessors – is that it is highly desirable that parties should make their intentions clear in any lease of a property that is adjacent to another vertically above or below it. It is, of course, desirable always to do so, but especially so when there are no presumptions to help.

Under the *Party Wall etc. Act* 1996, there are now such things as party floors and ceilings. Unfortunately, their existence doesn't help to decide ownership, but ownership may not matter quite so much when the apportionment of the cost of works to any party structure can be decided using the mechanism of the Act.

Previously, under the *London Building Acts*, the occurrence of horizontal party structures was limited, and this was because they were stated only to be within the definition when the properties were 'approached solely by separate staircases or separate entrances from without'. This meant that while the converted basement flat of a Victorian mansion might well have a separate entrance from, and thus a party ceiling/floor with, the ground floor flat, all the upper flats were likely to be reached via the original front door. In a modern block of flats, it might well be that none of the flats enjoyed a horizontal party structure.

A working party set up by the Pyramus and Thisbe Club (for a full description of this partly learned society of party wall surveyors, see *Anstey's Party Walls* in the same series) felt that this was an invidious distinction, and in drafting the new *Party Wall etc. Act*, declared that separate front doors were enough. The removal of the need for a separate entrance from the street cured a large part of the horizontal problem. However, even the existence of such Utopian conditions does not remove the advisability of expressing clearly the extent of any property being dealt with by sale or lease.

There are a number of exceptions to the general rule of *'cuius est'* with which this chapter commenced. Certain minerals are automatically reserved to various bodies.

Gold and silver, for example, belong to the Crown, following an Elizabethan (the First) case.

In addition, overflying is permitted by Act of Parliament. However, since *'cuius est, eius est'*, a crane may not be swung over a neighbour's land without his consent. Under the previous leading case on this matter, *Woollerton and Wilson v Costain,* the words 'which shall not be unreasonably withheld' were effectively added after 'consent'. In this case, Woollerton applied for an injunction to restrain Costains from swinging their crane over his land. Costains had offered all sorts of assurances and inducements to Woollerton, and the judge therefore granted the injunction, but suspended its operation for long enough to enable Costains to complete their works.

After this case, a nice balance existed. Developers knew that if they treated adjoining owners fairly, they were likely to be allowed to swing their cranes, and the neighbours knew that if they were unreasonable in their demands, they might find that they couldn't hold the builder to ransom. During this happy period, one 'crane' case came through John Anstey's hands. A grasping neighbour demanded £150,000 for allowing a crane to swing; John advised the distraught contractor to offer £5,000 in an open letter, with all the usual safeguards for the adjoining property, and to say that if this was rejected they would swing anyway, and see him in court. The grasping neighbour took the money.

In 1987, things changed. Anchor Brewhouses succeeded in obtaining an immediate injunction to prevent Berkley House from swinging their cranes over the plaintiff's land. The court affirmed the *'cuius, eius'* doctrine, but said, *obiter*, that there were strong arguments for limiting its upward application to a height that any reasonable man on the Clapham skyscraper might need for the proper enjoyment of his property. This may well be where the future lies, and in a further edition of this book, a lot of this chapter may be replaced by a statement to the effect that a man's rights in his property cease say, 20 ft (about 6 metres) above the topmost physical part of his building.

Until that day dawns, readers should note that we are not yet at the end of the story. In a recent case it was held that even quite low flying, for the purpose of aerial photography, could not be prevented – either as an act of trespass or on the grounds of invasion of privacy. It is this last case that gives some hope that the Anchor Brewhouses case might be reversed, and this chapter saved.

Finding the position of the dividing wall

What you are about to read may seem obvious, but knowledge of what is about to be imparted would have saved some litigants a great deal of money.

You want to find the position of the dividing wall between your house and next door, and the centre of that wall. We must assume, yet again, that the wall stands equally on the land of both parties, and that the boundary runs down the middle.

It is very easy to be confused in apparently simple cases, such as figure 17, by drainpipes which come down somewhere near the boundary line between the two properties. Sometimes a drainpipe is cranked near the gutter for the express purpose of reaching the ground on one side of the boundary, so as to allow a fence to be constructed in the right place. To be certain of the correct position, measurements are necessary.

If this is a joint exercise, and your neighbour is being co-operative, this will all be very easy, as you will be measuring inside and outside both houses, and checking each other's work. Usually, unfortunately, this sort of exercise is being carried out because both parties are already at each other's throats as a result of a disagreement about the position of a fence.

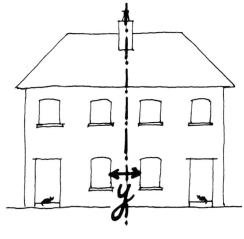

Fig. 17

Even at this late stage, it is strongly recommended that you approach your neighbour and ask to do the measuring before you erect or replace the fence. If you are on speaking terms with next door, and your houses are symmetrical, you simply divide the distance between the two nearest identical features, and the result puts you in the middle, standing on the boundary. You can check this by carrying out the exercise shown in figure 18.

Find the nearest convenient hole in your own wall, probably a window or a door in the rear or front wall of the house. Ideally, put something through it at right angles, i.e. parallel to the dividing wall. Measure from your marker to the inside face of the wall. Add on half an inch to an inch (12 mm to 25 mm) for plaster. This distance should give you the position of the brick face of the dividing wall. Now measure the same distance from your marker along the outside of the house, and you should have reached the same position: opposite the projection of the brick face of the dividing wall.

Now, if your neighbour's house is apparently symmetrical with yours, you can fairly safely assume that if you measure the distance between your respective doors (windows, or other holes), you will be able to ascertain the thickness of the wall. If you aren't friends with the neighbour, or if you don't want him to know you're carrying out this exercise, you may have to poke a measuring device over the fence while he's not looking (which is not a method that could possibly be recommended in this book), or much better, go out and buy one of those new laser gadgets that measure discreetly to a visible red dot. If you don't want to lean over, or it's too far, and you cannot afford a laser gadget, you can probably guess at a wall between 9 and 11 inches thick, and thus locate the boundary within an inch, working only from your own side.

If you can measure from both sides, Y – 2X = thickness. In other words, from the total distance between the openings, subtract twice the distance you measured to

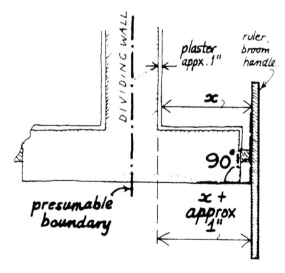

Fig. 18

find the face of the wall, and the result will be the thickness of the wall. The boundary, all other things being equal, will be in the centre of it.

If your houses are unbalanced (as most people think their neighbours are, let alone their properties), as in figure 20 overleaf, then carry out the exercise illustrated in figure 19. Again, this can be an easy joint exercise, or involve an assumption as to wall thickness.

In this case, the equation is $X - (P + Q) = R$, and the boundary is therefore either at $P + \frac{1}{2}R$ from the left-hand window, or $Q + \frac{1}{2}R$ from the right-hand door. (If you're lucky, it will be both.)

Once again, this may all seem obvious, but many are the cases that have gone to court where the contestants couldn't even agree upon this apparently self-evident starting point.

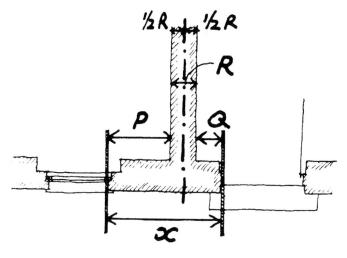

Fig. 19

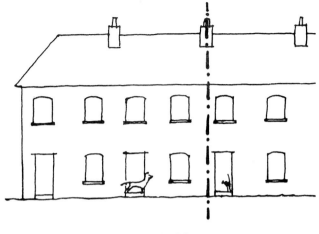

Fig. 20

There was a case in Harrow, for example, where the other side had pushed (literally) their garden shed across the boundary, right up against the neighbour's rear extension, which he had constructed so as to leave space for maintenance between the wall and the boundary. It took a county court action to persuade next door to pull their shed back to the 'party wall' line. in another case, where John Anstey sat as arbitrator, one side argued that a cranked drainpipe 'proved' that the boundary was more in their favour than the other side was prepared to concede. They appeared to have overlooked completely the fact that the drainpipe on the front of the house argued against them to exactly the same extent.

The position of the centre-line of the wall is of great importance when considering fences and walls in the garden (see the next chapter). It can also turn into a matter of grave importance with regard to the outside of a house. For some people, the horrors of their neighbour using stick-on stone cladding will make them battle for every half-inch of their boundary.

Garden walls, fences and bits of string

As has already been said in the Introduction, there is an awful lot of trouble to be found in suburban back gardens. In this chapter some ideas will be put forward as to how to solve many of the problems that give rise to the trouble.

Before we get to some 'matters of practice' for general guidance, it should be pointed out that physical clues can be equally – and perhaps more – helpful than a desktop study of the deeds in providing evidence of ownership in gardens, and from ownership you can often proceed to the position of the boundary. Go into the garden, look at the other walls, fences, or bits of string marking out the limits of the plot, and peer (without attracting attention) over into neighbouring gardens. If the rear fence and one of the side fences appear to be of the same date and the same construction, that is *prima facie* evidence that the same chap built and owns them. If a wall goes right round three sides of a garden in one style, it was probably put up by and belongs to the owner of that garden. If all the walls in a street have the buttresses on their eastern side, that tends to indicate that each house owns one wall, and its neighbour the other.

One leading authority, when asked for guidance on establishing the ownership of garden walls, replied: 'If it's in bad condition, it's next-door's.'

Now to some matters of practice.

There are a number of general practices or conventions regarding the building of walls and fences and how they relate to boundaries. Unfortunately, people being what they are, you will often find that suburbanites have ignored the practices in putting up their walls and fences, so that if you make assumptions based on generalities you will often be led astray. There are all sorts of exceptions to the practices, and to rush off to court on the basis of the practices alone would be extremely injudicious. Nevertheless, the practices must at least be considered, so that there is some sort of starting point.

If a garden wall has buttresses on one side only, it is probable that the wall belongs to the owner on whose side the buttresses are. The boundary is usually then the face of the wall furthest from the piers (figure 21(a)). If the wall has symmetrical piers, it is probably built astride the boundary, which runs down the centre of the wall (figure 21(b)).

When a fence is constructed of posts, arris rails and feather edge boarding, it certainly used to be the case that the face of the boarding furthest from the rails marked the boundary. The logic behind this was that the space between the posts remained in the garden of the man who constructed the fence (figure 22), and it also used to be said that it was proper for a man to drive nails (through the boards) towards his own land. The reverse

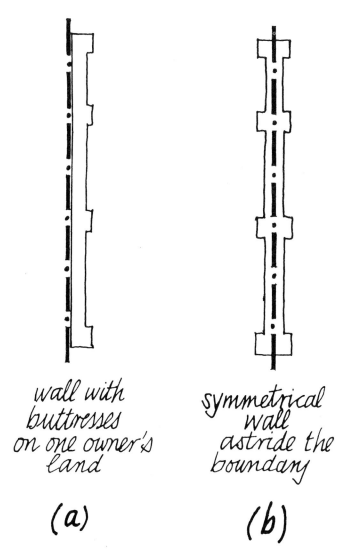

wall with
buttresses
on one owner's
land

(a)

symmetrical
wall
astride the
boundary

(b)

Fig. 21

logic of this is that you cannot construct such a fence, or repair it, without at least swinging a hammer over the land of your neighbour and that (see elsewhere), you have no automatic right to do.

69

Such fences can be described to their owners as being the opposite of curtains; with curtains, you have the pretty side facing inwards, and with close-boarded fences you have the pretty side facing outwards.

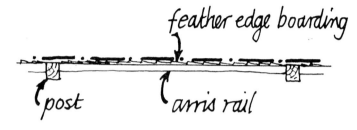

(a)   Plan of post & rails fence

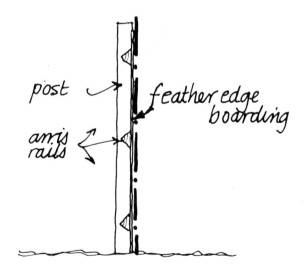

(b) Section through post & rails fence

Fig. 22

Larch-lap fencing is very popular these days and can be bought cheaply from garden centres and DIY stores. It looks, from a distance, as though it is the same on both sides, but if you take a closer look (figure 23), you will see that it is not. If you run your fingers lightly downwards, there is a smooth side and a bumpy side. The smooth side should face the neighbour's land (i.e., it should be on the far side of the fence-owner's land).

If a fence consists of posts and wire, it's very likely to have been erected on the boundary. The thinner the divider, the more likely – on the whole – it is to be on the dividing line (see figure 24). However, it is worth looking at the end posts of such a fence to check that the wire

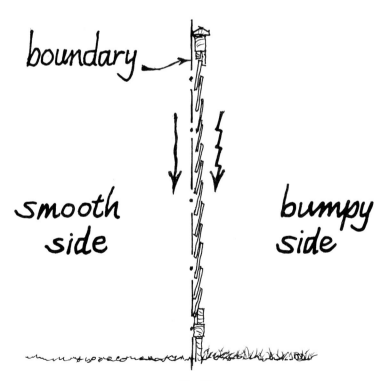

boundary

smooth side

bumpy side

Fig. 23

does start and finish in the middle of the posts. In some such fences, the wire starts on, say, the left-hand side of the start and end posts, but runs through the middle of all the intermediate posts. This is a strong indication that the fence belongs to and is on the land of the person who has the end posts on their side of the wire.

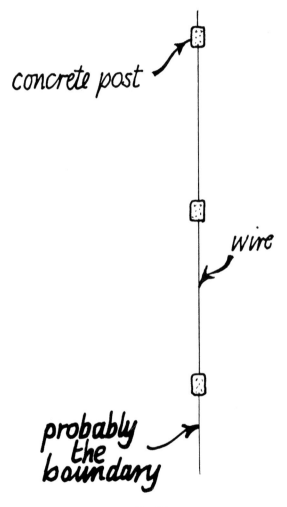

Fig. 24

That's most of the standard types of dividing wall (using the word loosely) that you're likely to find between back gardens. Of course, there are other types – pseudo ranch-fencing in plastic, woven panels supported in various ways, or concrete boards dropped into slotted concrete posts, for example – but you couldn't say that any of them have produced a presumption. Their position in relation to the true boundary will have to be deduced from first principles which, despite all the 'rules', is often the only safe way. This leads nicely onto a discussion of why some of the presumptions are unsafe.

One very good reason for not assuming without question that a boundary feature follows the general practice is that the person who put it there may not have been aware of the practice. Another is that the constructor may have known the rule, but deliberately not followed it for some reason. Circumstances may have dictated a non-standard solution. Let us look at some of the practices again, and likely eccentric variations.

A very simple, and frequent, deviation from the buttressed wall occurs when an unsupported wall starts to lean, and the party towards whom it starts to decline puts in piers to stop it going any further. These are usually fairly easily detected, as they tend not to be bonded into the wall, while piers contemporary with the wall usually are. Be warned, though, that the reverse may be true in either case, and that even when you have solved the dating question, you are still only dealing with assumptions.

Feather edge boarding is frequently to be found facing towards the man who owns the fence. He's paid for it, and he wants to see the pretty side. Besides which, he doesn't get on with the neighbours, and he can put it up this way round without going on to their land to nail the boarding. When this happens, there's almost always going to be a row, sometime, about where the boundary is. If our man puts the boarding on the boundary, most of the posts will be in the next door garden. If he puts the edge of the posts on the boundary, then when he's finished erecting the fence, a substantial area of his garden will be more accessible to his unloved neighbours. They'll be happy for now, but when he wants his land back for any reason, they won't be quite so accommodating (see figure 25).

Almost always, however, the reason that the fence and the boundary cannot be safely assumed to be correctly conterminous, or following the usual practices, is human fallibility. Save in cases of adverse possession, the boundary does not move with the fence, but fences move all over the place, with the effects of time, weather, handymen, and even fencing contractors. Very, very rarely – despite what your client will tell you – do the neighbours deliberately try to steal some of next-door's garden. But they're very bad at putting fences back where they got them from.

The best advice then, is: don't assume from presumptions and conventions; don't rely on anything that could have moved; don't believe anything that's been erected more recently than the houses; and work from fixed points wherever possible. Those fixed points are dealt with elsewhere.

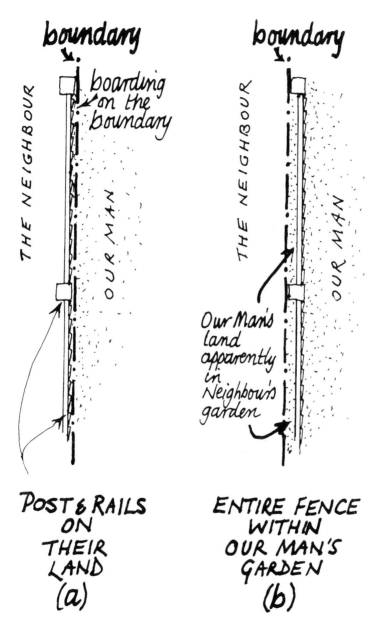

boundary

boarding on the boundary

THE NEIGHBOUR

OUR MAN

POST & RAILS ON THEIR LAND (a)

boundary

THE NEIGHBOUR

OUR MAN

Our Man's land apparently in Neighbour's garden

ENTIRE FENCE WITHIN OUR MAN'S GARDEN (b)

Fig. 25

Hedges (sometimes with ditches)

Many boundary disputes arise out of the practice, particularly in the suburbs of our major towns and cities, of planting hedges on or close to property boundaries. In the countryside there are also hedges with ditches, and these can likewise lead to misunderstandings.

It is worth having a brief look at how the Ordnance Survey (OS) deals with such features.

It is standard practice on OS maps, which are often used as the base for deed plans, for a hedge to be depicted as a solid line, indicating what the OS refers to as the 'rootline' (this can perhaps more easily be pictured as the 'trunkline'). In the absence of any other evidence, it can only be assumed in such cases that the hedge is a party-hedge (in the very loosest sense of the word 'party'). If it were possible to get into a time-machine and go back to the day on which the hedge was planted, you would almost certainly find that it was planted as a row of little twiglets on one side of a stringline (or an old wire fence) that formed the boundary. Zooming forward to today, we see a substantial hedge and no stringline or fence (it has long since disintegrated). The individual trunks of the hedge have almost certainly crossed the boundary, and although the hedge was once no doubt paid for and planted by one owner, it has now become the dominant feature separating the properties and straddling the boundary line.

In one recent case, the evidence on site was very confused, and included a holly hedge of considerable age and thickness. One side was attempting to argue that the far side of the holly hedge formed the boundary – at least where the hedge existed. Embedded in the hedge, however, was an iron fence that looked like the sort of (usually Edwardian) fence used to separate the immediate surroundings of stately homes from the farm lands adjoining. The wood of the holly had in places grown around the iron so as to enclose it totally. It seemed obvious, therefore, that the fence had come first, marking the boundary, and the hedge later, growing up around it, with no relevance to the position of the boundary at all. Later on, an early plan turned up which showed the pleasure grounds of a large house on one side of the boundary and a field on the other: this made the iron fence an even more likely candidate as the boundary marker.

Hedges such as this cause a huge percentage of suburban boundary disputes and are very difficult to resolve to the satisfaction of both parties. It should not be beyond the wit of a chartered surveyor in such a dispute to devise a hedge-management programme and get both parties to agree to it. Many cases regarding hedges occur where both sides are terrified that their neighbour is about to chop the hedge down; once they can be persuaded that this is not about to happen, a sensible agreement for the future upkeep of the hedge, with a clause covering its removal (if it goes past its sell-by date) with the written consent of both parties, can be drawn up. It may be hard work for the surveyor(s) involved, but it must surely be preferable to the parties going off to court and spending thousands of pounds of their hard-earned money.

With regard to the ownership of hedges on the boundary, your eyes are your best tool. One neighbour, for example, may prefer a different species of hedge to another. His garden might have a beech hedge planted around all four sides, with the neighbouring garden having a holly hedge around just three sides. This would be a strong indication that a disputed beech hedge would belong to the 'beech' house (see figure 26).

However, this is only a rough guide, as certain species of hedge (privet, hawthorn, leylandii) tend to belong to specific eras, rather than to individual properties.

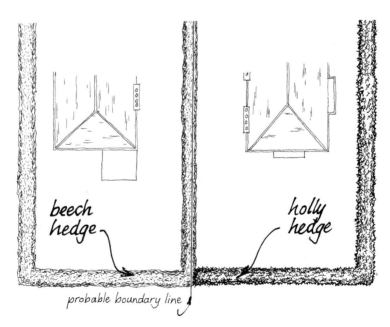

Fig. 26

Readers will be relieved to learn that in at least one set of circumstances, there is a firm (and indeed eloquent) logicality concerning hedges and boundaries in the eyes of the law. This is where hedges are accompanied – in one particular set of circumstances – by ditches. (It must be noted that in all other circumstances, the lack of a logical explanation means that other evidence must be sought.)

The firm presumption is this. Where there is a bank and a ditch between two properties, then whether or not the bank has a fence or a hedge on it (it usually does have the latter), the presumption is that a man has walked to the limit of his ownership, dug his spade in, and thrown the earth up on to his own land. The far edge of the ditch is therefore the boundary (figure 27).

For the hedge and ditch presumption to apply, the ditch must have been dug as the original boundary feature, with its main purpose being the marking of the boundary. If the hedge and ditch were once part of the internal

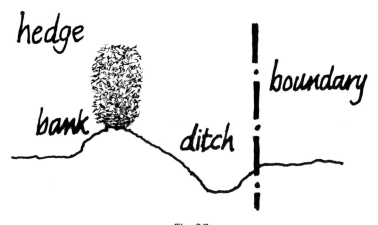

Fig. 27

layout of a large estate (with many fields), for example, which has more recently been subdivided and sold off, then the presumption will almost certainly fail.

Of course, in time the edge of the ditch (like the Rockies) may crumble, eating into the land of the neighbour, but it is unlikely that the amount of movement this would produce would be very significant in a field. It's not likely to happen in a suburban back garden, where a few inches might matter. (See Chapter 8, 'How large is too little?')

Where there is no bank, there is nothing to indicate how the ditch came into existence, and therefore no basis for any assumptions. If the ditch is quite clearly linked to drainage ditches or other features on one party's land, it might be reasonable, in the absence of contrary evidence, to assume that the ditch belongs to that party.

Talking of drainage ditches, there is a well-publicised case, still ongoing at the time of writing, where an owner instructed a contractor to dig a field drainage ditch inside his property (but close to the fairly vague boundary formed by an old fence), in which to lay a pipe. Shortly afterwards, a relation of the contractor bought the land next door, saw a few scrubby plants on her side of the newly dug ditch, and promptly took down her own fence and re-erected it on the far side of the ditch, gaining about 6 ft by 200 yards. While the opinions still being expressed by those involved in this case are strongly felt, there is no doubt that, at least in one respect, the contractor's relation was in the wrong – the hedge and ditch configuration has to be formed in one original operation; it cannot be created in stages at a later date.

If there are two banks and one ditch, one might argue that the ditch is a joint effort, and that the centre is the boundary. Where there is a single bank, with no hedge or fence upon it, and no ditch on either side, you might again advance the 'joint effort' argument, but you should also look for any other evidence. Again, there is no legal presumption if the bank is between two ditches, but common-sense would incline to the view that it would be reasonable to take the centre of the bank as the boundary.

Where there is a hedge alone, OS practice is to survey the middle of the hedge. However, there is more likely to be supporting evidence for the ownership of a hedge, although its outward growth may give rise to arguments about the exact position of the boundary in relation to it (as noted above). Such arguments are, on the whole, futile, and clients should be dissuaded from indulging in them whenever possible. A surveyor may find it expedient to advise such clients to find another adviser, where only a couple of inches are at stake.

With regard to ownership, if there are hedges on other sides of the land which were clearly planted by the same owner at the same time, then it is not unreasonable to assume that all those hedges belong to, and stand on the land of, the same owner.

In hedge and ditch configurations, it should be remembered that the OS usually shows just one solid line on its rural maps. This line, usually the centre of the trunkline of the hedge, is *not* the legal boundary where the hedge and ditch presumption applies.

Conveyancers and surveyors should also be aware of one hazard that exists when using OS maps to transfer land that has a valid hedge and ditch presumption at the boundary. This is shown in figure 28 below.

In figure 28 it can be seen that Owner A has land that reaches, using the hedge and ditch presumption, to the far right-hand side of the ditch. Owner B has land that extends (from the other direction) to that same point. Thus there is no conflict. However, Owner A then decides to sell to Joe Bloggs Homes, and his conveyancer, to make life easier, describes the land being sold as 'all that piece or parcel of land known as OS parcel No. 1234'. The accompanying plan will, of course, be an extract from the OS map and the line shown by the OS will be the centre of the trunkline of the hedge. In both places, therefore, in the text and on the plan, the land that has been sold is clearly to the centre of the hedge only, because that is the line on the map and is also the extent

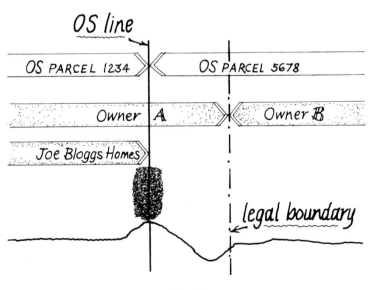

Fig. 28

of parcel No. 1234. This is a common occurrence and it actually means that Owner A, despite selling to Joe Bloggs and possibly emigrating to the Bahamas, is still the owner of half the hedge, half the bank and the whole of the ditch.

Where hedges (and ditches) are concerned, there is no substitute for using your eyes, not only to read the deeds, but also to assemble all the visual evidence. Then you have to apply your brain to put all the evidence together.

This chapter should perhaps be ended by saying that all these presumptions only apply where there is no positive evidence to the contrary. Even the best presumption – the bank and single ditch case – would be overturned by a clear statement in the deeds, especially in the deeds for the properties on both sides of the ditch, that the boundary lay somewhere else.

The empty garden

A tomb without a body in it is called a cenotaph; a wall without a window is said to be imperforate; what do you call a garden without a fence? This question is only asked because that would have made a better title for this chapter than the one that has been chosen. What is going to be examined is how you should set about deciding the line of a fence between two gardens, when there isn't one and you have been called in to advise on how and where it should be built.

The lack of a fence, wall or what-have-you, may have arisen in a number of ways. Perhaps the estate developer left it to the purchasers to erect a fence, and the two neighbours – or their children – got on so well together that they preferred to have the use in common of double the space. Now one or both of the original owners has moved, and the new ones would like their properties demarcated. Or perhaps the fence fell or blew down during an unpredicted hurricane – so thoroughly that its original position can no longer be ascertained with certainty.

Even if a former fence has left some posts or some post-holes behind it, there may be considerable debate about which side of the posts the boundary lies (see the chapter on Garden walls, fences and bits of string), or whether the posts are or were in the right place to start with (see the chapter on Adverse possession). However, with or without residual evidence, you're going to have to start somewhere.

If your client will allow it, the first thing you should do is talk to the owner of the garden on the other side of the missing fence. The importance of this has been emphasised elsewhere, but it must be repeated. If you can agree on the line of the fence before it is put up, there is less chance (though not none) of your being asked to take it down or move it later. For the purposes of this chapter, let us assume that your neighbour is ignorant but co-operative: he's not going to obstruct you, but he hasn't got any definitive help to offer.

First of all then, you should look at both deeds. With any luck at all, they will both be based on the same Ordnance Survey (OS) extract or estate layout plan (see the perils of relying on the same elsewhere in this book) and may even be the same plan, with a different part ringed in red. If that is the case and they look something like the next illustration (figure 29), your task should be fairly straightforward. In figure 29, next door (No. 25) bears the same dimensions and so, despite a healthy distrust of deed plan measurements, you can start from the fence with No. 21 and measure to the fence with No. 27, and see how close you get to 60 ft (c. 18.29 metres). If it's bang on, you can safely take 30 ft (9.14 metres) as your garden width.

But, as has already been stated, the centre of the party wall must be an absolutely fixed boundary – so what if the distance from the fence is not 30 ft to that point? Prefer the wall, but don't assume that the rest of the

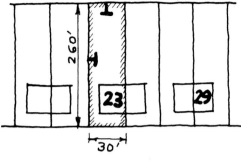

Fig. 29

boundary should necessarily shift by the same amount. In such a case, the best answer would be to divide the bottom of the gardens at the 30-ft mark (or as near to it as possible), and take a straight line from there to the centre line of the wall.

In the past few paragraphs, we have been thinking in terms of back gardens. Front gardens are often more tricky, because shared drives can make it more difficult to find a starting point for any measurement. You will have the safe starting point of the centre of the wall, though, and in a simple case you should be able to project it forward by triangulation, to continue the straight line of the wall. This does rather rely on the builder having set the house out squarely in the first place. Nevertheless, it is always better to relate measurements to a fixed point on the front boundary, if a reliable one can be found.

Ownership of the right-hand fence to No. 23 is almost certainly, in the case we're looking at, with No. 25. His deeds may show it, if they can be found, but the 'T' mark on the left-hand boundary implies it anyway. If there are no 'T' marks to be seen, you will have to wander a little further afield: viz., next door but one, two, and so on, to see if there is an established pattern of fencing to indicate ownership. Remembering that this is only an indication, you can nevertheless reasonably assume that if the nine nearest gardens all have the fencing facing one way, the missing one should face the same way and may well belong to the party to whom the standard assumptions would point.

You should, of course, look for indications on the ground: old fence-post holes and signs of attachment of the fence at the junction with the house and at both ends of the garden. These may be even more necessary when you are dealing with irregular boundaries between unequal plots.

Once again, if you can compare the deeds, do so. You may need to enlarge one or the other, and make overlays to compare or join them, but at least that is comparatively easy nowadays, with photocopiers that will do it for you to a high degree of accuracy – even if you shouldn't rely on 97% to mean exactly what it says as a reduction factor. If it is dangerous, by the way, to scale off a small deed plan, it is positively suicidal to do so off a photocopy. Don't even think about it.

If the gardens are irregular or steeply sloping, it may be worth calling a chartered land surveyor in with his car boot full of fantastic gadgets. Using a total-station (basically, a plain old-fashioned theodolite with a laser built into it, all packed inside a stylish case painted bright orange), a land surveyor can make a map of all the relevant existing features and download this onto a computer. AutoCad is the most popular computer software system for this purpose, but there are many others and, what is even better, after years of different computer systems not shaking hands with each other, they have now become promiscuous and shake hands with everything. You can buy a computer in London, software in New York, a printer in Cairo, a scanner in Buenos Aries and hey-presto they will all say hello instantly. There must be a song title in there somewhere.

A land surveyor can then scan in the deed plan(s) and match the two using a method known as 'best mean fit', which basically means fitting the two (or more) plans together in such a way that no matching feature is preferred at the expense of another. Nothing may match at all, but everything will match a bit. It is a skill that land surveyors use on a day-to-day basis and it is best to leave them to it. Co-ordinates can then be obtained from the resulting match and the total-station can be used in reverse to peg-out the line of the most probable boundary.

In such cases, it pays not to be too pedantic; if the high-tech land surveyor's line misses the stump of an old iron post by 2 inches, it is sensible to put all the wizardry back in the boot of the car and simply adjust the pegged line, proportionally, so that it passes through the said post.

In this series of Anstey books (see the cover for details of the others!), it has always been said that you must never put in print the fact that real experts know when to break the rules, because it encourages amateurs to do so when they shouldn't. It was with great reluctance therefore that John once had to admit to having scaled off some blown-up photocopies in an attempt to solve a boundary problem in Harrow on one occasion. (This is a different case from any others in Harrow mentioned in this book.)

Only one dimension was given on the plan, and virtually no measurements scaled from it agreed with any taken on site – including the one given. John therefore attempted to get some acceptable proportions from a big blow-up. They all bore some resemblance to each other, and to the facts on site. He didn't rely on them, however. Don't you.

When married, the two deeds should agree along the common boundary. If they don't, you have a serious problem on your hands, and you will either have to reach a friendly agreement with the neighbour, which should then be recorded on both deeds in legal form and notified to the Land Registry, or face the costly consequences. Failure to agree may produce the absurdly expensive legal proceedings that have been alluded to elsewhere. To repeat: it is better to give up a few inches of garden than to pay for several days in court.

When the overlaid (or scanned) plans agree, you still have the problem of identifying the boundary on the ground. Use every fixed point you can lay your hands on, and work from one to another as far as possible.

Lack of evidence is also positive assistance sometimes. In one case, it was possible to assert positively that if a fence had been fastened anywhere in such and such an area there would be signs of it. There were no signs, therefore the old position of the fence – and hence the boundary – had to be to one side of that area. Thus, the boundary was 'not to the left of point A'.

Sometimes there will be very little in the way of evidence on the ground. There were once two front gardens in Wembley, for instance, separated by a hedge. The deeds showed a boundary with an angle in it, but nowhere near enough measurements to be able accurately to fix the point at which the bend occurred (see figure 30).

On being called in, it was clear that 'they' had pulled up the hedge completely, leaving 'our' garage as the only point of certainty: the boundary was 'not to the left of' our garage. We had dimensions for the front of each plot, but neither of the opposite corners gave crystal clear starting points. Doing the best we could, however, got us to a more or less reliable point 'X'. From there to the garage we knew very little more than you can see in the diagram, but the further from the street the bend came, the better it suited 'them', as they might just be able to get a car past the house, which they couldn't with the hedge there.

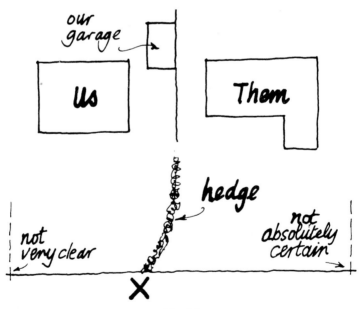

Fig. 30

Not for the first time, aerial photographs were of considerable assistance. Even quite obscure suburban properties may appear in such photos, and the cost of obtaining them can be much less than that of a day in court (see Chapter 7). The line of the former hedge could be seen quite clearly in the photographs, and it was not a difficult task roughly to trace its centre-line and then relate it to the two fixed points. It was possible to satisfy both sides – the neighbours being reluctant at first – as to where the boundary was, in relation to where the hedge used to be. It was even possible, by extrapolation from other ground features, coupled with those measurements that could be relied upon, to determine more or less where the bend came.

The more uncertainty there is on the ground and in the plans, the more important it is to stay out of court. If you can see that the issue is not clear-cut, you must realise that there is a case to be made for some other point of view. If you and your neighbour each find a surveyor to share your opinion, the two surveyors will both be subjected to lengthy cross-examination, and the result may well be a toss-up anyway. While the judge will sum up by saying, 'The true view is this', this means, as has already been implied in this book: 'I have heard a lot of argument; I don't understand half of it, and don't agree with the other half; what I think is....'

What a waste of money. Avoid it if at all possible, by reaching a compromise. If you have to give something, console yourself with the thought that you're probably getting something as well. And just think of all the DVD equipment, films, holidays in the sun and laser-measuring devices you'll be able to buy with what you've saved on legal expenses.

The task of the expert witness

An expert witness is a person who, through his qualifications, experience and knowledge of certain matters, is entitled to give an independent expert opinion on those matters.

David Powell, when serving as an expert witness, was once asked by a QC, during a pre-trial conference, 'How many cases have you won?' David replied correctly (and a little cleverly): 'None, I don't win or lose cases, I just give evidence.'

Experts operate in one of three roles nowadays:

- as an SJE (single joint expert);

- as an expert instructed by one of the parties;

- as an expert adviser.

In the first two cases, the duty of the expert is to the court. In the third case, the moral and professional duty is still present, but the expert's role is to give absolutely independent advice to his instructing client.

The idea of having SJEs came from Lord Woolf's team in the run-up to the emergence of the *Civil Procedure Rules*

(CPR) in the mid- to late 1990s. It appeared that a large part of the costs in a court case could be attributed to the enormous cost of using experts. In fact, this only appeared to be so to the lawyers; in the county court cases that David Powell has been involved in, typical total costs hover around the £15,000 mark (per party) and yet the typical total surveying invoices for those cases average out at around £3,000 (per party). While not wishing to criticise the admirable work of the CPR team, it is tempting to ask where they got their figures from.

The introduction of an SJE, appointed by the court and instructed jointly by both parties, has reduced the apparent costs, because there is just one expert, not two. However, in every SJE case that the updater of this book has been instructed in, each party has gone off and got their own expert adviser to make sure that their barrister can put the right questions to the SJE during cross-examination. As the costs of the new expert adviser are not recoverable and are not seen by the court, there is the illusion of a cost saving. However, the facts are that instead of two experts in court (the old system), we now have three and, even worse, the expert advisers are free from cross-examination because they merely sit in the shadows, with their post-it labels and scale rules.

Never mind; we are where we are.

If you are instructed as an SJE, there are excellent guidelines published by RICS and a plethora of seminars and conferences on the subject. In essence, it can all be stripped down to the following simple rules.

First, you must treat both parties in exactly the same way. You must copy all correspondence and knowledge of every contact with one party to the other. If you interview one party for two hours and 46 minutes, then you must give the other party exactly the same time, if they wish to use it. It is advisable, when measuring up the gardens, not to accept a cup of tea from one party, even on a cold misty February morning when the steam can be seen rising from the mug of Rosie Lee being proffered, because it will appear to the other party that you are biased. This is, of course, a matter of perception, but it must be observed if independence is to be seen to be maintained. If you are bursting to visit the loo, get in your car and drive to the nearest public convenience. If you are seen entering one property to visit their loo, the neighbours will view this as a complete capitulation.

The report (more later) must be sent simultaneously to both parties (or their solicitors) and, when written questions are received, the questions and your written answers must be sent back, to both parties, in the same post. If you send an e-mail, it must be sent to both parties (not sent to one and copied to the other).

The balance must be perfect.

When it comes to giving evidence in court, the role of an SJE is a lonely one. Wandering around the court building with his Tupperware lunch box, he is unable to enter any of the little rooms because nobody wants him in there. His lot is to sit alone on a bench in a nearby park – which, on second thoughts, sounds like something of an advantage!

In the witness stand, the SJE is pulled first one way and then the other, in two bouts of cross-examination – in which there seem to be no friendly faces. However, it should be remembered that there are very few judges who wake up in the morning, stretch their arms out and greet the dawn with the words: 'Oh good! I've got a boundary dispute today.' Not many judges go into the profession with a longing to deal with squabbling neighbours, and they do sincerely hope that the SJE is going to provide the answer as to where the boundary lies. The judge therefore is likely to be your one friend in court and will often help you out if nerves are getting the better of you and you start stammering when undergoing cross-examination.

The SJE role seems to be working, at the time of writing this book, although it will be interesting to see whether, given another five or ten years, a breed of rather self-satisfied super-experts develops, who have become lazy without the constant expert-examination that came with the old system. It really is up to you, readers, to make sure that this does not happen, and that the role of the SJE remains professorial rather than superficial.

There are still many cases, of course, where each party appoints its own experts. One such expert, only a few years ago, was heard to say, 'he who pays the piper calls the tune'. This is the exact opposite of what should and must take place. The client is paying to receive independent warts-and-all evidence and it would be a complete disservice for the surveyor to tell him simply what he *wanted* to hear. That would be like consulting a doctor who always tells his patients that they are fit and well, even when they plainly aren't. Experts must be brave enough to tell their clients when they are wrong. It is better to incur the wrath of an angry client than to see that client spend thousands of pounds chasing a hopeless goal in court. Not only that, but to do otherwise opens the surveyor up to being sued for breaching RICS guidelines, breaking the CPR, and generally being a bad sort.

Where two experts are instructed, one by each party, there should be a simultaneous exchange of reports, followed by a meeting of experts. This will usually be ordered by the court. The result should be a list of agreed and disagreed points and, most importantly, an agreed plan (more on this subject later).

The expert report must be a stand-alone document and must be addressed to the court. It should contain the following sections, although not necessarily in this order (experts can retain their own style, while still conforming to the RICS guidelines and the CPR):

- a title sheet;

- an index;

- a mini-CV;

- a copy of your letter of instruction;

- a brief description of the problem;

- a brief description of the surveying methodology;

- an analysis;

- a conclusion;

- maps, plans and photographs.

It is always greatly appreciated by the court if the surveyor remembers to number the paragraphs (for easy reference) and uses double spacing (to allow barristers to write cross-examination notes and comments between the lines).

The mini-CV is essential in that it shows the court that you are the right expert for the job. It is no good being an expert in valuing houses and trying to convince the court that you are the right person for a boundary dispute. Similarly, it does no good for a land or building surveyor to put himself forward as a valuation expert: it's horses for courses.

With this in mind, there follows a special message for land surveyors. It is one of the mysteries of life that most land surveyors are congenitally shy. They come from the ranks of quiet children who play on their own in the corner of the garden: they are the boys who support the school rugger team rather than star in it; they are the girls who read *Swallows and Amazons* rather than go out clubbing. The only major film featuring a land surveyor, *The Englishman Who Went Up a Hill But Came Down a Mountain*, starred Hugh Grant in the leading role. It should be borne in mind that most land surveyors could adequately be played by Hugh Grant, and therefore their CVs are likely to be short and understated. A retired land surveyor who had been in charge of a major survey of part of the Ganges Delta in India was once heard to say, blushing as he did so, 'Oh yes, I think I was involved in a spot of measuring overseas once.' While this attitude plays well in the Army & Navy Club, it is not really what the court needs. The court wants to know that you are the right expert for the job and that you know what you are doing. Bashfulness will give the wrong impression.

On the other hand, the section on methodology should be short and sweet. The idea is to tell the court how you did the survey and to what degree of accuracy it can be relied on. It is not the opportunity to describe how a Cooke Troughton & Sims theodolite is made or how many millimicroseconds it takes for a total station to measure a distance.

When it comes to the analysis section, the important thing is to picture the process as if it were an experiment at school. The updater of this book, David Powell, remembers his schooldays of the 1950s, when discipline was harsh and, every Tuesday morning, there was double chemistry. Pupils sat at a big table doing some unfathomable experiment involving test-tubes until milk break. Milk break involved consuming a small bottle of warm milk (it had been left out in the Birmingham sunshine for an hour or so) and a slab of lardy-cake (the cake that launched a thousand calories). After milk-break, the pupils trooped back to their desks, opened their rough-books, took out their 2-B pencils and wrote up the earlier experiment. It is a discipline that still holds good when writing reports today, providing a break between the physical and written tasks and thus allowing ideas to crystallise in the mind. The maps, plans and aerial photographs replace the test-tubes, a cup of Nescafe's finest takes the place of the milk, a hobnob supplants the lardy cake, and the laptop computer ousts the rough book. Nevertheless, the sequence remains the same. Try it; it works.

Then there is the conclusion. Make sure it concludes. This doesn't mean that you have to come up with a definitive answer; you can be vague, but be vague in a definite way. If you think you know, from your analysis, where the boundary lies, then say so, clearly. If the outcome of your analysis is that there are several options, then say that you simply cannot say where you think the boundary lies and state that clearly too. You may then go on to discuss the 'most probable' boundary line. But avoid writing a report that is so vague and hedges so many bets that it mystifies the legal profession and is of no use to anyone.

Remember that boundary disputes that go to court rarely have simple answers. If the answers were simple, the case probably wouldn't be in court anyway.

A judge in Lincoln County Court in a case where John Anstey was the expert for one side and David Powell the expert for the other, announced to the court halfway through that 'trying to determine this boundary is like trying to construct the skeleton of a prehistoric monster from a huge jumbled heap of bones.'

Harking back to the meeting of experts, it cannot be overstressed that it is not a meeting of surveyor-advocates. So many of these meetings involve at least one of the surveyors trying to fight their client's case for them. That is not the purpose of the exercise. Experts should meet as though they were both sitting together trying to solve the *Daily Telegraph* crossword. They are both doing their best to find the answer and, working together at such a meeting, they may get a better answer than working separately. It is certainly not a case of 'who is the best surveyor?' It is perfectly possible for experts to disagree over crucial matters; there is nothing wrong with that. Hence the 'disagreed list' ordered by the court. Similarly, the agreed plan should not represent an opportunity for one surveyor to show off to the other that he possesses better laser equipment. The agreed plan should be neutral in authorship (being a combined plan), with just the two signatures and the date on it.

It goes without saying, of course, that no lawyers or clients should be present at the meeting of experts, and that the meeting should ideally take place on neutral ground, preferably indoors and away from the properties in question. The reasons for this are that if the meeting is held on site, it will be just a matter of time before one of the parties comes out and tries to join in. Another reason is that it usually pours with rain at the very moment that the experts wish to spread out their respective plans and photographs. If a site visit is required to check some disagreed point, then it can be a joint swoop onto the site at the end of the meeting.

Appearing in court can be daunting. The bit that frightens experts is the cross-examination, and this is a natural fear. Once you enter the witness box, you are alone, and the cross-examining barrister will use his skills to try to take your evidence to bits. That is what they are paid for, and once you have taken this on board, the whole experience should not be so frightening. Remember that experts are seen as being fair game by barristers, and you should expect a rough ride. The way that you cope with this is to be prepared for everything you can think of. Have your favourite calculator in your pocket, your trusty scale rule to hand, some coloured pens and blank paper for explaining things with, and reply to the judge – not directly to the questioning barrister.

Never, but never, argue with a barrister: they will always win – they do it for a living. While you are measuring and photographing every day of your working life, they are arguing and testing. If they test you to the extreme, they are simply doing their job; it is not a personal thing.

One of the best things to picture when you have taken the witness stand is that there are two beings in there. The first being is your evidence and the second is 'you' the person. A barrister will probably accept (privately) that your evidence is good and unlikely to be dislodged; however, the 'you' bit is (because we're human) full of flaws, contradictions and fears. Hence, a clever barrister will try to attack the 'you' bit, and then, having made you quiver like a jelly at a five-year-old's birthday party, will hope you will go on to make a mess of your actual evidence. Recognise this technique, and you will almost certainly find the experience easier.

Other obvious bits of advice include speaking slowly and clearly; admit getting things wrong (you may say east instead of west out of nervousness); and ask the judge for clarification and help if you do not understand a question being put to you or if you feel you are being bullied.

Finally, one last bit of advice from John should always be heeded. He was a great believer in having a last-minute revisit to a site before a court case. He was absolutely right, of course – it is amazing how such a revisit clarifies the issues and features in your mind before taking the witness stand.

Clients in court

Do not let clients give evidence, if you can avoid it. It is their case of course, and there may be factual matters, or historical ones, on which they have to go into the witness box. However, as all boundary disputes tend to have strong effects on the participants, the parties can become over-emotional when giving evidence and damage their own cause. All surveyors know that their jobs would be easier to do if only clients weren't involved, but in boundary cases the adverse effect of this factor is at least doubled.

Big cases are usually much easier to deal with than little cases – and the size and standing of the clients is highly relevant, too. If Marks & Spencer meet Sainsbury's across a disputed boundary, they will appoint experienced surveyors and will, in all probability, accept their advice. The whole matter, involving city land worth hundreds of thousands of pounds, will be settled in a short time, between level-headed boards and their professional advisers.

John Anstey was once involved in a discussion (it was not a dispute: no one knew the facts, and both parties were united in their wish to reach an amicable and equitable solution) between a large foreign bank and a major land-owning charity. Between their two properties was an ancient wall, which clearly pre-dated both of the current buildings to which it was party. The bank was redeveloping and wanted to use this opportunity to agree a boundary with the charity, so that the bank could build to that boundary now, and the charity later, without any future difficulty.

Both sides appointed competent surveyors, and the first thing they did was to commission an extremely accurate survey of the party wall. This produced an extraordinarily shaped thing, in both plan and section, which has been roughly reproduced below (see figure 31).

To the absolute delight of the surveyors, they discovered that there was one plane that could be drawn through the whole wall and that never stepped outside its thickness in plan or section. This was fixed on as the boundary. The clients instantly agreed, and then all that had to be done was to have the solicitors enshrine this in a legal document. Explaining it to and teaching them was a different matter, but they got there in the end.

Let two suburban neighbours dispute which side of a fence post the boarding should be nailed, however, and you may be in for months – if not years – of ill-natured wrangling. One at least of the parties – not your side, of course – will have appointed an incompetent surveyor to advise them, or no surveyor at all. The incompetent may be the wife's brother-in-law (who's a quantity surveyor), or a clerk from the Borough Surveyor's office, or even a qualified surveyor who is so scared of offending one of the three paying customers he has at present that he daren't contradict them in anything, and certainly has no intention of applying his own powers to try to find out the truth of the situation.

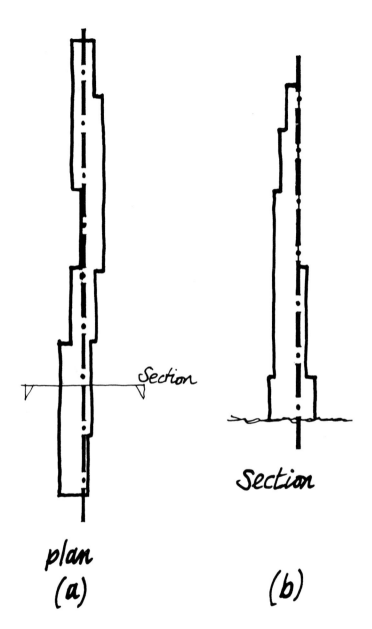

Section

Section

plan
(a)

(b)

Fig. 31

It is very rarely that such disputes stop short of arbitration or the courts (mediation being a forlorn hope in most cases). It would always have been cheaper, in such cases, for one party to pay the other for the disputed land – and often cheaper for one of them to move to another house to get away from the scene of the disagreement. Vain though the effort be, you must try to persuade your client (the sensible one) of the truth of these remarks, and endeavour to get him to cut his losses.

If no powers of persuasion are of any avail, and the two parties cannot be brought to agreement, or even to a compromise in which both of them think themselves equally hard done by, then you must train your client in the art of giving evidence. (See the chapter on expert evidence for general remarks on the subject.) Impress upon your client how important it is to stick to the subject of the dispute. Do not let him tell the court about the time when next door poisoned the roses.

John Anstey was once involved in a noise case in west London which was lost by an individual on the other side conducting his own case (when his expert's opinion was not unfavourable to his cause). He would insist on going over the planning history, emphasising how wrong it was that his neighbours had ever been given planning permission for the extension from which the noise emanated. Every time the Clerk of the Court dragged him back to the point, he would say, 'Yes, I see. Well, in 1972 when they applied for...' If he had kept his mouth shut, or better directed and relied on his expert, it is possible that he might have won. As it was, he so exasperated the court that John was able to clock up another resounding triumph.

Even experienced experts have impossible clients, however.

John was at one time involved in a case in which (unbeknown to him) his client had earlier attacked an offending fence with a sledge-hammer, leading to her being bound over to keep the peace. He did know the lady in question well enough to beg the solicitors to keep her out of the witness box, arguing, what could she add to my technical evidence? It's her case, they replied, and she wants to give evidence. John was cross-examined for two hours and held firmly to his opinion. Then the client stepped into the box. 'It's like the Berlin Wall' (which, at that time had just been built), she emoted. 'I don't promise I won't attack it again with my little sledge-hammer.' End of case.

Clients! Stay away from them. Keep them out of court. Keep them out of the witness-box. End of chapter.

Mistakes and pitfalls to watch out for

Do not think that authors are infallible. It is well known that, if you read a newspaper report of an event which you attended, you will hardly recognise the matters described as being those which you witnessed. Something is not necessarily so because it is enshrined in print, and the authors of this book are not always right.

Still less should you assume that pundits never make mistakes in real life. They should, on the whole, get things right in a book, because another knowledgeable person will usually have checked the text. Only a very obstinate writer will persist in error, without at least pointing out that there is an alternative view. When you are actually involved in a case, however, it is not always easy to get an authoritative check on your opinion: the best person to go to – the one whom you would ask to read your manuscript if you were a writer – may be on the other side.

A mistake should be seen as an opportunity to learn, and thus avoid it a second time. Some of the mistakes that the authors of this book have made (perhaps that should read 'that the authors know they have made') point a general lesson. Some just point out how easy it is to err. See below for details.

In a built-up area, when you are looking at the facades of two adjoining buildings, there is often a clear-cut division between the two: one may be faced in brick, and the other in stone. The boundary is therefore obviously the line of junction between the two. Oh no it isn't. There are all sorts of reasons why one or the other material may project across the boundary. Just one is that the stone facing may mask the joint between the two properties, in order to produce a more elegant effect (see figure 32).

A party wall award (if one happens to exist), or some other such agreement between the owners, may well record the true boundary, and perhaps state that the adjoining owner may cut off the projecting stonework if he needs to do so when he comes to redevelop.

A rather more excusable error is almost the reverse of that case, but in some ways parallel. You may be able to see a straight brick joint between two facades, and therefore assume that there are two walls behind the joint.

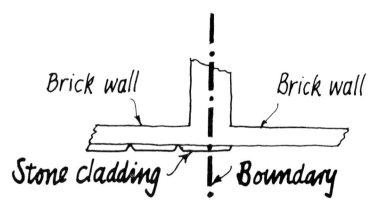

Fig. 32

Not necessarily there aren't. Very often the joint has only been put there to give an apparent dividing line, and it does not reflect either the existence of two walls or the boundary. To make this mistake (see figure 33) can be very embarrassing when you start to knock down 'your' building. This happened to one of us on the site where the *Estates Gazette* office now stands.

We have to admit that neither of us personally made the next mistake: the other side did, but we might well have done if our client hadn't pointed it out to us.

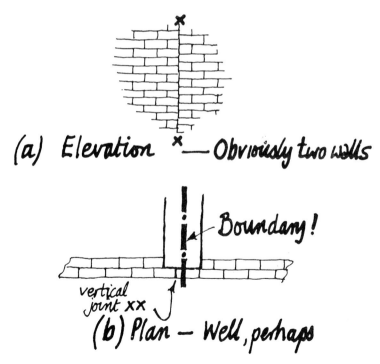

(a) Elevation *— Obviously two walls

(b) Plan — Well, perhaps

vertical
joint xx

Boundary!

Fig. 33

You might assume that if you are in possession of the plan of a newly developed group of plots, and the dimension from the outside of your wall to the boundary is shown on the plan, then whatever next door says, that dimension must be correct.

Well, not invariably it mustn't. On the plan in question in this case, the distance from the wall to the boundary was shown as 2 ft, but then so it was on the other side of the line. The distance between the faces of the two walls was only 3 ft, 9 inches. Either wall might be in the wrong place, or the boundary might still be equidistant from both. It turned out, for a very obvious reason when you looked closely at the facts, to be the latter. The plans showed both houses built with 4½-inch brick outer skins. They had in fact both been given 6-inch stonework outer skins. The inner skins and the cavities were placed exactly where they were shown on the plan, but that meant that the space between the outer faces had contracted.

Solid objects, such as houses, garages, garden sheds, greenhouses, and so on, are not likely to take up their beds and walk. When you find a fence, therefore, erected later than a substantial tool shed, underneath the eaves of the shed, and where the eaves were formerly within the curtilage of the shed's owner, you can safely assume that the fence is trespassing.

Oh no you can't. John was once dismayed, having made that assumption, to hear the fencing contractor say that he and his gang had shoved the shed aside in order to erect the fence, and had then shoved it back again – just too far. Fortunately, this did not destroy the basis of the expert evidence (the case was in court at the time), although it did move the line a little. How was John to know that the shed could move? Answer: by looking a little more carefully at how solidly it was fixed to the base.

If you are looking at a series of Ordnance Survey (OS) maps, ranging over 100 years or so, and in all of them the corner of the garden of No. 49 High Street is in more or less the same position, even though its shape varies a little from year to year, it is only reasonable to assume that it hasn't moved. That obviously then provides you with a fixed point from which other boundary features can be measured.

Oh no it doesn't. It may do, but unless you have made overlays to ensure that the garden has not been enlarged by purchase from neighbouring landowners (or other means), you can't be sure. It came as a very nasty shock to one of us when we were asked by counsel, in cross-examination, to lay a 1969 map over a 1938 one. The difference in size of the two gardens, and the movement of the corner that was being relied upon, was too great to be explained away as a variation in free-hand drawing.

As in the last case, this did not destroy the conclusions, but it removed the absolute certainty that had been claimed for one of the starting points.

In another case, a lady in Shepherd's Bush phoned John and said that her neighbour insisted that the front fence should be at a right angle to the house. She disagreed. 'Silly woman', John thought, 'of course it should be at a right angle.' 'What about the deeds?' John asked, 'Do they show an angle?' 'Oh yes', she said, and John thought, 'The silly woman can't read deeds either.' She insisted that he come to look, and off he duly went.

The deeds showed that not only hers, but the six or so adjoining houses also had boundaries at a funny angle, and the fences showed this on site. Clever woman, Miss Eagle, and she and John became very good friends. Clients aren't always wrong, so look at everything with an open mind.

We have warned you elsewhere not to assume that you can rely absolutely upon legal presumptions. We would refer you back to the chapter on 'Garden walls, fences and bits of string' to review that warning, but also repeat it here. Indeed, we would go further: never simply assume anything. Check, look, read, think and then conclude, but always state what assumptions you have been forced to make in order to arrive at your conclusion.

It causes us some distress to observe that this chapter is so long – and we haven't even told you, since we're not writing about rights of light, about the time when one of us was completely deceived about the age of a window, so skilfully had it been moved from one position in a wall and matched into another.

Let's end with one last mistake along the same lines. On this occasion, one of us was shown an old gatepost by a farmer in Matlock, Derbyshire, and when the farmer was asked, 'How old is it?', replied, 'At least 60 years old'. This gatepost was then used as one of the starting points and was photographed and described in great detail in the expert report. It was on the morning of the trial, some ten minutes before David (for it was he) was about to take the witness stand, that the farmer whispered to him... 'You know that post? It's true that it's over 60 years old, but I only moved it to where it is now a couple of months ago...from the other side of my farm.' A very embarrassing start to David's evidence ensued!

It is some consolation to be able to use the errors of our (relative) youth to warn our successors against following in those particular footsteps, but even more to reflect that the court cases described still resulted in complete victory for our clients. Despite the incorrect assumptions we had made in each case, our general conclusions were upheld and our drawings of the boundary lines were accepted.

However, take heed, there is truth in the old adage, 'nobody likes a clever-dick!'

Conclusion

It has been said – probably too often already, but that isn't going to stop it being repeated – throughout this book, that if there are just three words of advice about boundary disputes, they are these:

Don't have them.

If there is a point of doubt, consult before acting. 'Agree with thine adversary quickly, whiles thou art in the way with him', rather than ignore him until he serves a writ. (No doubt some readers are by now gratified by that other Biblical quotation: 'My desire is...that mine adversary had written a book'.)

It is never, never – well, hardly ever – worth going to law (or arbitration) about a small piece of garden; most unlikely to be worthwhile doing so about part of a field; and seldom, if ever, done about city centre land. A stitch in time of friendly discussion – which is what almost invariably happens in the last sort of case – saves nine poundsworth of fees.

Those remarks are really addressed to the people who own the boundless or disputed land. Now, turning to the surveyors who may be called in to solve the problems.

114

Don't hesitate to disagree with your client. If you don't think his case carries weight, say so. He will rarely thank you for saving him from vast expenditure, but you will have the satisfaction of knowing that you have done so.

Use your eyes in every direction. Ask for documents. Ask again. Examine the evidence. Don't limit yourself to the immediate confines of the plot. See if there are nearby comparables that will help. Use the local library for early Ordnance Survey (OS) maps. Ask the local newspaper for any relevant photos. Don't jump to conclusions.

Don't be afraid to say that you don't know. Say what you do know, and express the limitations of what you can only guess at, while indicating how well-founded your assumptions are.

When you are absolutely certain that you have formed a correct view, when your client has understood and agrees with it, and when he fully appreciates how much even successful litigation is likely to cost him, but is still determined to go to court, then you should read the chapter on being an expert witness, so as to give him the best chance of success. Even better than that, however – and this really is the last time you will read it in this book – would be to persuade the neighbours to agree or, failing that, to compromise.

Boundary disputes always profit lawyers; usually profit surveyors; never profit the owners.

Index

Note: Bold figures indicate whole chapters